Praise for *Storytel*

110628505

"Renée Damoiselle has not just created a
teller but turned it into a system of spiritual and magical transformation.
Storytelling Alchemy is a must for anyone who wishes to follow the path of
the storyteller but also wants to take it just that little bit further."

—Janet Farrar and Gavin Bone, authors of *A Witches' Bible,*
The Witches' Goddess, The Inner Mysteries, and *Lifting the Veil*

"An enjoyable and informative read about the magic of storytelling.
Whether you're looking for inspiration for your writing or for your life's
journey, *Storytelling Alchemy* will guide you on an adventure of discovery
into untapped wells of mystery, magick, and motivation."

—Melanie Marquis, author of *The Witch's Bag of Tricks* and
Modern Spellcaster's Tarot

"Grab your sword and your shield or rather a gorgeous pen and a journal
that speaks to you, because *Storytelling Alchemy: Write Your Own Happy
Ending* by Renée Damoiselle is a beautiful, engaging, and fulfilling book
that seeks to train men and women to fight their own battles where it
counts—in their memories. It is empowering, the storytelling appealing
and attainable. You can't wait to see what you'll write!"

—Amy Blackthorn, author of *Blackthorn's Botanical Magic*

"Our brains process information through stories, but what our conscious
mind often forgets is that we can create these stories. Renée Damoiselle's
Storytelling Alchemy reminds us of that and helps us make these tales
magickally work for us."

—Lilith Dorsey, author of *Love Magic* and
Voodoo and Afro-Caribbean Paganism

"It has long been known by the wise that we are made up of stories,
as much as we are of atoms. No doubt, you've been in the presence of
a great storyteller that held you rapt within a tale seemingly more real
than the room you sat in. There is a storyteller more powerful than the
best you've heard, and they are always with you. It is the voice of your
mind, your soul, that shapes the flow of meaning in your life. *Storytelling Alchemy: Write Your Own Happy Ending* teaches you how to become
awake, aware, and capable of using this magick that is always present
within you."

—Ivo Dominguez Jr., author of *Keys to Perception:*
A Practical Guide to Psychic Development

STORYTELLING

Alchemy

WRITE YOUR OWN
HAPPY ENDING

RENÉE DAMOISELLE

WEISER BOOKS

This edition first published in 2018 by Weiser Books, an imprint of

Red Wheel/Weiser, LLC
With offices at:
65 Parker Street, Suite 7
Newburyport, MA 01950
www.redwheelweiser.com

ISBN: 978-1-57863-638-9

Library of Congress Cataloging-in-Publication Data available upon request.

Cover design by Kathryn Sky-Peck
Cover photograph by iStock
Interior by Deborah Dutton
Typeset in Adobe Garamond and Proxima Nova

Printed in Canada
MAR

10 9 8 7 6 5 4 3 2 1

This book is dedicated to Constance Ann Martin. Mom, from the moment I could write, you told me I had talent. You listened to my endless stories and always complimented my writing. You lived in a way that I wanted to emulate and your encouragement, support, and love have helped me to write my own Happily Ever After. I love and miss you.

CONTENTS

ACKNOWLEDGMENTS

There are many who deserve my thanks and appreciation for helping me throughout the writing and publishing of this book.

First, I would like to thank you, my dear readers. Without you there would be no reason to write, and since writing is my passion, life would be terribly dull without you!

A big thank you goes to my love and life partner, John M. Becker. You've always helped me to feel that taking the time for my creative endeavors was a good thing. You never made me feel like I was neglecting "us." You've given me all the encouragement and support that I needed, but my favorite thing is the look of pride that you have when you see what I accomplish. That fills my heart with joy. I love you!

These acknowledgments would not be complete without thanks to two amazing women in my life. The first is Maggie Esposito, my beautiful, wise, and wonderful daughter. You've been such a great cheerleader and inspiration to me. You are the whole reason that I have strived to improve myself. I've known for a long time that your children don't grow up to be who you tell them to be; they grow up to be who you are. I've tried to be someone I would want you to emulate. You've exceeded my expectations, and our relationship is so gratifying and soul-filling for me. Thank you for being there with a happy and hopeful look on your face at the lantern festival where I wrote down my intention of publishing a book and we set the lantern aloft with fire. Dreams do come true. And having a daughter like you is a dream come true for me.

I must also acknowledge Maria Bird. My dear friend, my *anam cara*, you have carried my heart, mind, and soul through all sorts of changes and adventures! You were part of the inspiration for this work, when you brought people's personal stories into our rituals at Odyssey Ridge.

For Bernadette Montana, my High Priestess, my teacher, my surrogate mom (even though you're too young to be my mom), you've always challenged me and simply expected me to live up to my potential. No fussing, no cajoling, just "Do this thing." You pushed me forward with such confidence in my abilities that there was no room for my own doubt. Thank you.

There are so many people who have given me encouragement and shared my excitement in this process. I thank you all, and I'll simply provide a list, though not exhaustive and in no particular order, of the people who've helped me to persevere through this process: Ellen O'Brien, Roze DeFabis, Roxanne Torre, Chuckie Betancourt, Sally Piotrowski, Daniela Hoffmann, Christine Malapanis, Nicole Wherry, Teresa Hall, Michael Kuehn, Val Rivera, Robert Mullins, all of the visitors to Witch in the World's Cottage, and too many others to name. Thank you!

I have to give a special shout-out to Miriam Yoeman, my dear friend and coven sister. You were one of the kindest, most loving, wise, intelligent, and giving people I've ever met. I miss you more than I can say. Thank you for your example and for the friendship and love we shared.

Finally, I'd like to thank my editor, Judika Illes, who gave me the chance to fulfill a dream of publication and then walked me through every step. Your kindness, wisdom, and experience have made this process joyful!

INTRODUCTION

We all have a story. We've all experienced tragedy, challenges, and darkness. And when we continually hold that story in our mind, retelling it and thinking the tragedy through over and over, it becomes a part of the psyche. In fact, it casts a spell on us.

Whenever we experience difficulty, our emotions have a way of storing the beliefs generated around the situation in our unconscious mind so that, even when we are not consciously aware of it, we will continue acting on those deeply held beliefs. The problem is those beliefs formed in tragedy, pain, and sadness are almost always false.

These deeply held beliefs must be uncovered and made conscious in order to remove their hold on our lives. Your personal story—the story you tell yourself about who you are—can halt your progress in life, keep you from forgiveness, and stop you from reaching your true potential. Your story—whatever that story is—should empower you, not limit you.

I've written this book to help you transform your limiting beliefs into empowering ideas. Letting go of the past is never easy, and this book is no quick fix. You will be challenged to examine your past, your excuses, and your limits. You will discover techniques that will enable and empower you to work for your freedom and enlightenment—the way it should be. Utilizing these techniques can change things for you in ways you've not even imagined.

There are two ways to approach this journey:

- This book can serve as a simple self-help guide for uncovering your unconscious blocks and moving forward with powerful new ideas about yourself.

- But this book also contains magick. If you are new to spell-casting, you will find some very practical beginner tools in these pages. If you are a seasoned witch, you may find yourself challenged to take your workings even further or deeper.

One of my earliest teachers in witchcraft was fond of saying, "The first thing that magick changes is the Self." I've taken my own journey on the Storytelling Alchemy path, and I will share that with you. You'll learn from my successes *and* my mistakes.

My childhood—like many others—was not ideal. There were events from the early part of my life that used to limit me, including abuse, rape, and alcoholism. These were my realities. But storytelling allowed me to see the Truth beyond the reality. Through storytelling I began to see my own part in all of my darkness. Writing stories helped me to take responsibility, change some of my false but deeply held beliefs, and move toward freedom.

I began the practice of storytelling intuitively, but since my first foray into the world of fairytales and happier endings, I've studied with experts on the topic of reaching the unconscious. I've read countless books and attended dozens of seminars and classes on the process of human transformation and the workings of the mind. I also trained for many years one-on-one in an initiatory tradition of witchcraft and studied and experimented with spellwork for most of my adult life. Perhaps my love for magick and my willingness to believe in its effectiveness sprang from all of the lovely fairytales of my childhood. As a practitioner of witchcraft, I incorporated spell-work into my recovery and healing. I worked hard—and still do!—to uncover the Shadow side of myself, and this continues to help me to this day.

I've condensed all the knowledge and experience I have accumu-lated over the years with storytelling, alchemy, and "the magick that changes the Self" into this book because it has been such a valuable practice for me, and I want to share that with everyone who can benefit from the lessons I've learned.

The following pages are packed with writing exercises, medita-tions, prompts for reflection and self-examination, and dream anal-ysis, as well as spells, enchantments, and spirit offerings to help you along your journey.

I've been teaching these techniques in workshops since 2010 and find it so rewarding to see the changes my students experience. This book is a way to reach a larger audience and help more peo-ple to overcome their own darkness and reveal their inner wisdom and light.

How would your life change if you could let go of the past? What would be different for you if forgiveness became your norm? How would your decisions evolve if you truly believed yourself to be limitless?

Being able to act from a place of compassion and understanding for yourself and others is a profound catalyst. Being able to take back your personal power and consciously manifest your own future is bliss.

My life has transformed from one of resigned duty to limitless possibilities. The practice of Storytelling Alchemy has given me the ability to see that everything is possible for me now.

One of my students shared with me that during her work in my class, she realized one of her most limiting beliefs—that she was "not good enough"—came from an incident in grade school. With the techniques I taught her, she was able to uncover something previously hidden from her conscious mind that was keeping her from exploring her true potential. The incident, in which she was "the last one chosen," might seem insignificant on the surface—who hasn't experienced that?—but once she uncovered and examined the emotions and the ideas that had implanted in her subconscious from that experience, she realized its hold on her. And when she started writing about it and adding a new perspective, she began to change that deeply held belief about her inadequacy. And that is a powerful transformation.

Don't wait to create your own transformation. If you're reading this, that means something inside of you is eager for change.

If you are willing to delve into your own past, psyche, and stories and look closely and fearlessly at your life to make positive changes, this process will help you turn your leaden, heavy, dark past into the golden, bright future you desire and deserve. That's alchemy for you. Lead to gold, baby!

Come with me on this journey. Be your own hero and take this leap with me. I will be there with you every step of the way.

Read on and I will reveal to you a portal to your own inner wisdom. Trust me, it's there! The journey on which you're about to embark will help you intuitively and naturally turn all of your "Once Upon a Times" into "Happily Ever Afters." And this transformation takes place whether you believe in magick or not.

CHAPTER 1

TWO PATHS FOR YOUR JOURNEY— MUNDANE AND MAGICKAL

What do I mean by *mundane* and *magickal*?

This book will give you plenty of solid, step-by-step instructions for actions that you can take in the "real world" to bring to life your new story and your new perspective. These actions are grounded in what we call the "material world." That is the mundane. *Mundane* means worldly. Some of the instructions for this practice involve the ordinary legwork it takes to accomplish anything in this world, such as reading, writing, or recalling memories.

If you take every mundane step laid out for you in this book, you will create an empowering new story, your perspectives will change, and you will gain a deeper understanding of yourself and your world. All of that is mundane: take these steps; realize that result.

But there will be another aspect to the work in these pages that you may not have considered before. I am a practitioner of magick. Some, myself included, would call me a witch. And I have found over the years that combining some good, old-fashioned, solid leg-work with a little bit of practical magick can speed the work along and vastly improve my outcomes. Some of the magickal workings that you will discover here include the material world. You may use objects such as incense or bowls of water for offerings. There will be physical acts to perform when practicing the magickal parts of Storytelling Alchemy. But these physical objects and actions are connected to *an energy* that we hope to influence in our favor. The actions of magick are intended to put universal laws of nature in alignment with our intentions, which takes them to a higher level than just plain mundane legwork.

In this book, I'm using the spelling *magick* with a *k*. The British occultist and author Aleister Crowley first coined this spelling to dif-ferentiate the practice of casting spells from stage magic, prestidigi-tation, or illusion—true magick from tricks. There are no illusions in magick. In fact, in my experience it is instead a way to uncover and open the mind and psyche to what is real and true. You may also see me refer to witchcraft and spellcraft. Although arguments could be made regarding the differences between these terms, in this book I will use them interchangeably.

At the beginning of this chapter I mentioned the "real world" to give some description of what I meant by *mundane*. If *mundane* means "worldly," then does *magickal* mean "otherworldly"? And what is "real"? Let's explore these ideas for a moment.

The current scientific worldview most of us are familiar with tends very much toward the philosophies of materialism. If we can't see, touch, hear, smell, or taste something, or if we can't trace the connections mechanically, then it's considered "not real" and rele-gated to the realm of imagination. If something can't be measured and quantified, today's western scientists reject it.

However, there was a time on our planet when magickal thinking was the norm. People did not know the origins of natural phenomena, such as an eclipse or an earthquake. This was all magick to them. If you took a flashlight back to the year 1000 BCE, you would be worshipped as a god. But, because science has been able to determine the causes and connections for how a flashlight works today, it is now "real" and mundane.

Ignaz Semmelweis (1818–1865) was a physician working in a hospital in Hungary during the 1840s. This hospital had a high mortality rate of about one in ten for mothers during childbirth. A nearby hospital had a much lower rate of one in twenty-five. Semmelweis set out to discover what was causing this difference. He noticed that in his hospital staff would go directly from working with cadavers to delivering babies without washing their hands and suspected that cleanliness might have something to do with it. At the time, no one knew about germs and bacteria that could spread infection.

Semmelweis implemented a protocol for doctors and midwives to wash their hands before each contact with a new patient. As a result, the birth-mother mortality rate dropped to one or two in 100. But despite these good results, his idea was contrary to the standard thinking of his time. Even though bacteria and germs were and are real things, science had not yet identified them, and since the connection between cleanliness and healthier patients couldn't be quantified with the means available, it was rejected. Furthermore, many of his fellow physicians were offended by the suggestion that they were unclean and potentially responsible for these deaths. Semmelweis's handwashing protocols were rejected by his peers. The medical community branded him a crackpot, and he was disgraced. His contract with the hospital was not renewed. Eventually, he was committed to an asylum, where he died unrecognized for his pioneering work. It was not until decades later that scientists like Louis Pasteur began to prove that germs can be spread in unsanitary conditions. Imagine how many lives could have been saved if Semmelweis's colleagues had embraced his theories?

I've gone off on this tangent just to give you an example of how people with new ideas have been treated by the established scientific community. When connections between things are invisible to the available scientific tools and experimental methods, those connections are seen as imaginary, even if they are later proven by better technology.

Today science has shown us that everything is made up of energy, and the practice of magick is about recognizing and manipulating energy. However, the word *magick* still carries with it connotations of the supernatural. This is not how I view it. In my understanding of the universe, everything is connected. I believe that everything we do and say and even *think* has an effect on the world. The ripple effect on a pond is one example of how our actions can influence things that are distant. But I believe the connection goes much deeper—or rather, much farther—than that.

I've been using the word *imaginary* as something scientists treat dismissively. If something is imagined, it doesn't exist, right? Yet, we have this noun *imagination*, so *something* must exist. Every person on the planet understands what it is to imagine, even scientists. Can we truly be certain that the stuff of imagination exists only in the mind of the imaginer? This inner world that each of us can attest to having is defined as *consciousness*. The interesting thing about consciousness in the world of science is not just that science has not yet been able to explain what it is; science, western science especially, has largely just ignored its existence altogether. It's easier that way because consciousness seems to be wholly indefinable by our current scientific means. And those few scientists who might put forth the idea that consciousness should be studied are chided for being philosophers instead of scientists.

The philosophers do have their theories, of course. One of them is called *panpsychism*. The idea behind panpsychism is that everything has consciousness—from humans and other animals all the way down to plants and crystals and the earth itself. In my mind, understanding that everything we know is made up of some indefinable energy sparks a question. What if everything *is* consciousness?

Stay with me here, I'll not lead you down *too* deep a rabbit hole. Science has discovered ever-descending building blocks of the world as we know it, such as molecules, which are made up of atoms, which contain electrons, neutrons, and so forth. What if we've not yet discovered what it is that makes up those subatomic particles? What if that something is, in fact, what we call consciousness? And what if it's all connected in that way?

Science has proven that subatomic components exist in both wave form (which is a nonmaterial energy) or particle form (which is matter as we understand it). The experiments that discovered this fact also led to the realization that the waves or particles correlated to what the observer or experimenter wished or expected to observe! Perform the experiment expecting to see waves and you see waves. Perform the experiment expecting to see particles and you see particles. It's called the observer effect.

Now, most physicists don't delve into the philosophy that this discovery might bring up. Theoretical physicists prefer the math, not the philosophy. But to me, what is science for, if not to explain the nature of reality? Once the math is done, shouldn't we delve into what it all means? The so-called hard sciences may not wish to consider the philosophies behind the math, but witches do! Well, at least this witch does!

At the subatomic level, things behave very differently. There is, apparently, no objective reality. And the observer influences the experience. The first thing this shows *me* is that we humans have the ability to affect the building blocks that make up all of the world that we know.

Furthermore, an experiment performed in Geneva, Switzerland, in 1997 showed that twin particles or "entangled" particles—particles which had previously interacted physically—could have an instantaneous effect on one another from a distance of seven miles. The experiment manipulated one photon of light and proved that its entangled partner seven miles away behaved exactly the same way in exactly the same moment. Theoretically, this instantaneous communication between the particles is not expected to be diminished by distance. In a recent experiment in China, one of the entangled particles was sent into orbit around the planet with the same result!

Magick is simply a purposeful manipulation of energy—or perhaps consciousness—intended to bring about a desired outcome. Brain waves are particles with electrical energy. Science can detect our brain waves by measuring the electrical impulses firing within our brains. Thoughts appear to have electrical value or power. Thoughts are things. In the practice of magick, we train ourselves to arrange our thoughts in a specific manner, with the idea of effecting a specific outcome or with the idea of imposing our personal Will on reality.

So, our Will is involved in the spell. Now, what if we add some physical items to aid in the practice of arranging our thoughts in a certain way? All humans develop associations. We associate things with ideas: Gold represents wealth. A butterfly represents transformation. A mountain represents strength. We are constantly surrounded by real things that double as symbols for ideas. These symbolic associations are a way of engaging and uniting the unconscious mind with the conscious desire.

The magick that I perform—some of which I will share with you in this book—utilizes thoughts, written words, physical objects, and ritual actions to create a thought (an energy!) that is powerful enough to effect change on my world.

I don't believe in the supernatural. I believe we witches are simply skilled at manipulating the energies that already exist in nature to help us manifest our Will.

You may have noticed that I've used the word *Will* with a capital *W* a couple of times now. And, as you can imagine, this means that I am talking about a very specific definition for this word. I found this definition at OxfordLearnersDictionary.com: "Will: noun—the ability to control your thoughts and actions in order to achieve what you want to do; a feeling of strong determination to do something that you want to do."

When I use the term *Will* in relation to practicing magick, it includes this intent, but it also encompasses the concept of a very focused desire or intention and control over not just your thoughts and actions, but also the energies of the items you use in your spell.

My understanding of the word *Will* is also connected to a concept put forth by the famous high magician Aleister Crowley, which he called "True Will." True Will encompasses a lifetime. It is akin to life's purpose. When I perform magick, I am practicing in line with what I believe to be my True Will.

Please know that what is written here about Will and True Will are extreme oversimplifications of Crowley's philosophy, and if you want to know more, I suggest you research further. Begin with *Liber AL vel Legis* aka *The Book of the Law*. This book is now in the public domain and can be found in its entirety on www.sacred-texts.com. Then follow the rabbit hole from there if you feel inspired. I just want you to have a basic understanding of what I mean when I use the capitalized word *Will*. It's powerful far beyond what most people think. Having the *will* to resist dessert when you're dieting is great. But having the *Will* to change the world is something else entirely.

Now that you have a minimalist primer on the ideas both magickal and mundane, let's move on to storytelling and why both paths will be useful in this work.

Storytelling is usually seen as a mundane practice. Anyone can pick up a book and recite the words and deliver the story. Many people can also make up a scenario and roll with it until a story emerges.

But some storytelling, under certain circumstances, can be very magickal. Think about how powerful words can be. Witches use incantations or strings of particular words to cast spells. Imagine the power of a whole story delivered as an incantation.

Just consider this quote from the Gospel of John (King James Bible):

In the beginning was the Word and the Word was with
God and the Word was God.

Many take this to mean that "The Word" created the world! I believe this. Think about it: Nothing has ever come into being in the world as we know it without first having been *thought*. Most of us think in language. And certainly language is a way that we can take what we think and usher it into the world to create our reality. Using words in a very conscious and purposeful manner while putting the power of one's Will behind them creates reality as we perceive it. If that isn't magick, I don't know what is!

I'm not here to convince you that magick works. You'll have an opportunity through the practices of this book to find out firsthand.

All this scientific discovery and explanation of how I understand things might prompt you to ask, "Is magick real?" And I would say to you, that perhaps a better question is, "Is magick useful?" And the answer to that is a resounding yes! The word *real* can be interpreted in a number of ways. But if you get the results you want by using magick, who cares if you can define it as "real"? It gets the job done. I hope you'll include it in your Storytelling Alchemy work.

Alchemy—a magickal term for transforming lead into gold—can also be used in a mundane way. Many take the practice of alchemy as a kind of philosophy that has the purpose of transforming the philosopher through learning and discipline. It is a quest for enlightenment. We'll get further into the practices and ideas behind alchemy later in the book, but, for now, just keep in mind that profound transformation is the purpose of the exercises you are about to learn. Be ready for it!

Know also that the story you choose to tell may be rendered in words or any other form of creative expression. Your thoughts, your words, your emotions, and your creativity will birth this project into the world. This book includes specific instruction and advice for creating spells, altars, and sacred space and powering your own inner magick. Many of the exercises are designed to clarify and focus your personal Will in order to give power to the spells we will perform.

If you are new to spellcraft and magickal workings, I encourage you to add that to your mundane work. And if you are an experienced witch, you'll know that the combination of the two paths will bring your work more power and therefore bring *you* deeper transformation. For magick, first and foremost, changes its own practitioner.

So make your choice about how much of the teachings of Storytelling Alchemy you'd like to incorporate. As I said, you *will* effect change in your own personal story by sticking to the mundane exercises if that's what you choose. But I promise that there is nothing scary in the magickal workings I'll present to you. You are not opening the doors to demonic possession or conjuring spirits from the ether. You are simply utilizing energy to help yourself *become*.

Become what, you wonder? Become powerful, become sovereign, become wiser, become more comfortable in your own skin. If those sound like things that you want, give it a try.

This will be an expedition into your heart and mind and soul. And you wouldn't want to embark on an expedition unprepared. In the next chapter I will outline some tools that you'll need and explain their purpose. You will pack your knapsack with those things that will help you throughout your Storytelling Alchemy journey. Read on to begin your preparation.

CHAPTER 2

SEVEN ESSENTIALS FOR YOUR TOOL KIT

Think of this chapter as an orientation. Here you will find suggestions for how to begin and what tools you'll need for your journey. The information here is intended to get you into the right frame of mind to accomplish what you're setting out to do. Parts of your task in changing your story will be whimsical, fun, and enjoyable. Other parts will include intense soul-searching and taking a hard look at your past. I want you to be ready for all of it, with presence of mind and a plan that will carry you forward. So, in this chapter, I will outline the tools you'll need, some of which will be actual physical implements for the practice of Storytelling Alchemy, but others will be some foundational lessons that will serve you as you read through this book and perform the exercises and create your new story. Some other tools and items will come up later for certain parts of the practice, and I will make those suggestions as the need for them arises. But here I offer you seven tools to employ throughout your Storytelling Alchemy journey.

And speaking of your story . . .

THE STORY YOU TELL YOURSELF

Everyone has a story. In fact, we all have multiple stories. For example, each of us has "The Story of My Life" that is epic and grand and presumably still unfolding. But "The Story of My Life" is made up of many smaller stories that include everything from "My Childhood" to "My College Years" to "My Eighteenth Birthday" to "My Trip to the Store." You see, all the memories you hold on to of what has occurred in your life are stories.

I'm being a bit repetitive because I want you to begin thinking of these events as stories. Some of them are very positive and come with happy endings. Some are tragic and sad. Others are comedic, and still others, rather neutral. But the fact is that our collections of memories and our personal history may be viewed as many individual tales.

For the purpose of the practice you're about to learn, I want your first tool to be your mind-set. Stop thinking about your personal history and your memories as fact. The *fact* is that your understanding of these happenings is extremely subjective because of the emotional factors involved. (Remember, there is no objective reality!) Each individual story of your life is what I like to call the Story You Tell Yourself. I'll be referring to this throughout this book as the SYTY. This is not in the least intended to belittle the things that have occurred in your life or to demean the emotions attached to them. The purpose of referring to the SYTY this way is to provide you with a frame of mind that allows for change.

When we actively dig into our memories, we tell ourselves these stories over and over again.

Some of these stories are happy; some are not. The ones that tend to be harmful, and the ones that we want to transform, are those that produce the harshest feelings in us. Sadly, human beings tend to cling to the negative, and most of us have been in the habit of repeating those tragic or difficult stories to ourselves.

Each time we relive those memories of harmful events in our minds, we are perpetuating the hurt. The SYTY feeds a feeling of righteousness, self-pity, or justification. It is always emotionally charged and viewed from your side only. It is, therefore, also skewed from objective reality. You've heard the expression, "There are always three sides to a story: his side, her side, and the truth." And Shakespeare said, "There is nothing either good or bad, but thinking makes it so."

The SYTY does indeed include facts. The events really did take place. But we almost always include our own narrative when recalling our stories which inevitably speaks to our opinion of it and our emotions around that. How we *think* about the past determines how we feel about it and, perhaps most important, how it affects us in our present.

There is another aspect to this relating to the unconscious mind. The SYTY is one way that you may be sabotaging your own power, but there is another aspect to the psyche that may have a much stronger hold on your daily decisions and the way things play out in your life than you realize. And this is the unconscious and deeply held belief. These are the kinds of beliefs parents, teachers, mentors, and peers implant in our minds, usually unintentionally when we are at a very early age. These are very troublesome aspects of our psyche, precisely because they are unconscious. We're not aware that we are acting on those beliefs in our daily decisions, but suddenly we find ourselves wondering how we got into "this situation again."

Here's an example. A little girl is repeatedly called "ugly" by her big brother, whom she loves and admires. This is reinforced when the grown-ups in her life tend to talk about how beautiful her sibling is and never seem to mention her appearance at all. This girl grows up and in her adult life is plagued by the idea that she must be unpleasing to look at. She cannot leave the house without makeup. She prides herself on intellect and actually develops a disdain for beauty and those who value it. She doesn't consciously know why she chooses not to go to this or that party. She has no conscious awareness of why she accepts any romantic advance as a pure miracle and therefore lands in relationships where she is mistreated. She is hindered in many aspects of her life by this deeply held belief.

The truly insidious aspect of the deeply held belief is that when you have one, you constantly look for proof it's true. Your subconscious mind prompts you to seek out and collect statements, events, and ideas that "prove" this view of yourself. So the young woman in our example will seek out situations where her looks will be judged, measured, and found wanting, even if she isn't consciously aware of it. She will assume that when a suitor gives up on a relationship with her, it is because he found someone "prettier." She will notice people staring at her in public and assume they are engrossed by a morbid fascination with the grotesque.

Our unconscious mind is a very powerful motivator in our daily decisions, and it will seek to reinforce its beliefs at every turn. If its beliefs are true and empowering, then all is good. But if those beliefs are false—such as "I am ugly"—decisions will be made based on that lie, and the courses of lives will be altered because of the decisions made with respect to it.

What we *believe ourselves to be* becomes the rudder of our lives.

There are also things that are *true*: she was told she was ugly. And then there is *Truth* with a capital T: she is not ugly.

Let's try another example. A story from ancient India also demonstrates the point I'm attempting to make here.

This story is about six blind men trying separately to identify an object from feeling it. The first man declares the object to be a wall; the second, a rope. The third man said he felt a pillar, and the fourth, a tree branch. The fifth blind man said he encountered a great fan, and the sixth swore it was a spear. When they compared notes, they were astonished to find how different their descriptions were and could not come to an agreement as to what it was they actually encountered.

What they all tried to identify was an elephant, but each blind man was able to perceive only one part of it. The man who perceived a wall was feeling the side of the great beast. The man who perceived a rope held the tail. The pillar was the elephant's leg. The tree branch was its trunk, and the spear was the elephant's tusk.

Each man's description was *true*, but the elephant was the *Truth*. Perspective has a lot to do with it. And we all have our own perspectives relating to everything that we experience. Those perspectives are invariably based upon our experiences, our understanding, our limitations, and our deeply held beliefs.

I attended a seminar years ago where the speaker asked anyone in the audience who considered themselves to be a patient person to stand up. I think I'm patient, so I stood up. Then, he asked all the folks who considered themselves to be *impatient* to raise their hands. They did so. Then he asked the impatient group why they labeled themselves as such. The answers ran the gamut of things like,

"I can't stand to wait in line. I get agitated and tap my foot or fidget."

"I hate it when a traffic light is too long, and I count the seconds until it turns."

"I want the outcomes of my work to manifest instantly. It drives me crazy when they don't."

Then the speaker requested, "All of you patient folks—any of you who have been, thought, felt the same way, raise your hands." And every single one of us who considered ourselves to be patient raised our hands. Every. Single. One.

What this demonstrates is that how we *think* of ourselves is purely subjective and therefore subject to reframing. It showed the people who thought of themselves as patient that they could sometimes act in ways that would be considered impatient. And the people who labeled themselves as impatient saw that their actions in certain circumstances did not necessarily mean that particular label fit them any better.

This should show us all that any limiting belief you have about yourself is 1) probably false or at the very least extremely subjective and therefore open for debate; and 2) subject to change through your future thought process.

The purpose of this book is to reframe the most difficult of the SYTY in a way that allows you to shed the burdens of fear, anger, resentment, shame, and grief attached to it. This book contains exercises, meditations, and practical instruction for making the changes to your thinking that will set you free. You will be rewriting at least one SYTY as a fairytale. We will refer to that rewrite as Your Fairytale.

Throughout this book, I will refer to writing and/or rewriting. However, once again, subjectivity comes into play here, and this time it's mine! Writing happens to be my default creative process. What I really mean by *rewriting* is *re-creating*. This process and practice are open to whatever *your* creative process happens to be. Your final creative project may manifest as a sculpture, a painting, a musical magnum opus, or a dramatic performance. Hell, it could manifest as a beautifully decorated room or an amazing tank full of fish! Be open to the various directions your creativity takes you. There's no wrong way to tell a story.

But no matter how you decide to tell your new story, first you need to organize your thoughts. So the next tool is important.

YOUR STORYTELLING ALCHEMY JOURNAL

The first tool you've been given is the mind-set of holding the idea that your story is alterable in a favorable way. The second tool I want you to employ is a journal. You will create your main story in whatever medium suits you, whether that be handwritten or word processed on a computer or in another creative medium of your choice. But you must have a journal constantly at your side throughout your practice of Storytelling Alchemy. The word *journal* has the same root as the word *journey*. The etymology of these words takes us back to the word for *day*. Keeping a journal is meant to be a *daily* practice. Your journey will progress day by day. It is very important that you are able to keep your Storytelling Alchemy journal close by at all times and I'll explain why.

You will record many different ideas, inspirations, lessons, and exercises in this book. It is important to keep these insights in one convenient place so that when it comes time to review, you have one cohesive record of your thoughts and experiences. Throughout this book, you will be prompted to do writing exercises and to record some memories from your past.

Your journal may include drawings, writings, clippings from magazines, or photographs. Add to it whatever you find relevant to this journey. Add stickers, locks of hair, and pressed flowers if they have significance for Your Fairytale. Your storytelling journal will be a significant part of the process described in this book. I also believe it will be a valuable and beautiful way for you to look back later. Think of it as a keepsake and treat it that way.

Feel free to take up your journal and write down any musings you may have along the way. Your insights about your progress, memories that you uncover, and your thoughts on the content of this book are all valid candidates for entry into your journal. All of this will become relevant to your journey. You never know where inspiration will strike! And remember, anything goes. If you are out and about and come upon a scene that reminds you of a SYTY, take a picture and then print it and place it in your journal. It all counts.

A note about your journal: Choose one specifically for Storytelling Alchemy. Also think about employing a special pen for this endeavor. And please don't scrimp on your journal and pen. Find a journal that is beautiful and special, and seek out a pen that you love. You must love the look and feel of the pen and the way that the ink flows. You should view your storytelling journal as something unique and really pleasing to you. Your journal and pen will be your constant companions throughout your transformation. Your pen shall be your magick wand and the journal, your book of shadows or grimoire. Specially designated tools become sacred. Over time you will find that picking up your journal and pen will trigger a contemplative state for your mind and get you ready to move forward with your alchemical journey.

MEDITATION

Yes, I admit it, dear reader: I'm tricking you into beginning a meditation practice under the guise of writing a cool story about your life. The fact is that I want this practice of Storytelling Alchemy to reach your soul, and I know of no better way to do that than with our third tool of meditation. So, this book will include several exercises that require you to become still, aware, and meditative. There will be instructions for visualizations to be done in a meditative state designed to move you toward your intended goal. I confess my ulterior motive, but I'm not ashamed. I believe this practice will assist you to find your freedom from past hurts and be a boon to your everyday life in all respects.

I suggest making meditation a regular practice in general. I will say here that I credit meditation with being the single most important factor in saving my life—yes, I actually did say, "saving my life." It took me out of deep depression and anxiety, complete with nightmares and panic attacks, to a life where my gratitude is flowing in a continuous stream throughout each of my days. I am living a happy, fulfilling, enjoyable life. Of course, there were other factors in my transformation—like storytelling and magick—but meditation was, and continues to be, the *most* helpful. Perhaps I'll write that book for you one day, dear reader. But here I will teach you a couple of specific techniques to help you reframe the experience of the SYTY through meditation, which should be an ongoing practice to help support you in your transformation and spark your imagination for the development of Your Fairytale.

Meditation is also a magickal practice. There is no exercise I've ever found that increases my ability to focus as efficiently as meditation. As we discussed earlier, the making of magick requires a powerful Will, and a powerful Will requires a focused mind. All of the tools in your Storytelling Alchemy tool kit will help you improve that focus and empower your magickal workings.

RITUAL

It's best to work on Storytelling Alchemy as a "ritual." The simplest definition of the word *ritual* is a series of actions done in the same way and in the same order each and every time it's done in accordance with a certain protocol.

Although many will see the word *ritual* and think of a religious ceremony—and that is fitting as well—we enact many rituals in our lives. They can be as simple as making your morning coffee every day. We tend to call such things a routine or a habit, but if you think of them as a ritual, they take on a bit of sacredness.

One of my morning rituals is having a glass of lemon water. When I head into my kitchen after waking in the morning, I go to the cabinet and choose a glass. I place the glass on the counter. I open the refrigerator and reach for my bottle of organic lemon juice. I pour a very precise amount from the bottle into my glass. I watch the liquid flow and listen to the sound as it splashes into the glass. Then I return the bottle to the fridge and close the door. I notice the slight breeze of chilled air as I do so. Next, I turn to the corner of my kitchen with the purified water cooler and place the glass under the spigot. As I turn on the flow of water to fill the glass, I wait for the air-displacing bubble that rises in the water tank. I watch and listen. When my glass is full, I close the spigot, raise the glass to my lips, and take a long refreshing drink.

All of this is done mindfully, in full awareness of the present moment, and in the same way every morning I am at home.

That's a ritual.

The meditation practice taught in this book is another ritual.

I will also instruct you in a ritual practice of regular offerings to Spirit. As used in this book, the capitalized *Spirit* can be interpreted as a divine or universal energy of some kind or an archetypal idea—such as the Warrior or the Wise Man—or purely a psychological construct that allows your mind to better focus on the task at hand. It could also simply be a way to acknowledge and connect with your own highest wisdom, your own creativity and your best self. Lowercased *spirit* or *spirits* would be for a divinity of the land where you live, saints, sages, angels, or teachers of the past.

Why is ritual the fourth tool in our tool kit? You may, throughout the exercises in this book, recall memories that are challenging and even painful. The framework of ritual and meditation provides a safe place from which to confront these memories. The ritual and the meditation are themselves a pleasant and enjoyable experience.

One of the things you'll need for performing your rituals is . . .

SACRED SPACE

The word *sacred* means holy or consecrated; devoted or dedicated to a particular use; a sanctuary. Setting aside an area of your home to practice Storytelling Alchemy will serve to help you focus on the task at hand each time you perform the exercises in this book. Additionally, any sacred space gains energy and power from each ritual carried out within it, so each time you return here to meditate, write, make offerings, or organize your thoughts, you will be adding power to the place itself. And that power will, in turn, provide energy for the work you do there.

So how do you create your sacred space?

First, figure out the best place to work on your Storytelling Alchemy. Will you sit at a large table and write longhand? Will you be seated at a desk in front of a computer? Perhaps a sunlit room would facilitate your visual art creation. Another consideration for your sacred space is where you'll feel comfortable and safe and the atmosphere is pleasing to you. It's best if this can be a separate room, so you can close a door and have time to yourself. If that's not possible, choose a corner or a nook, but try to separate it from your usual daily activities as much as possible.

Remember that you are giving *to yourself* in this process. The act of setting aside the space and consecrating it is part of the gift that you are receiving when you invest in self-improvement. Accept the whole gift with open arms. It is an essential beginning to the changes you desire.

Once you've chosen the location, you can begin to make it sacred in a process known as consecration. You will begin by thoroughly cleaning the area where you'll be working. This should be a deep cleanse. Clear everything away and wash down or dust and polish surfaces. Organize the items in this location in a pleasing and uncluttered way. Do not think of this process as a chore. Stay present in the moment as you clean. Be aware that you are preparing a setting for your personal transformation. It's important. Your thoughts, your patience, and your attention to small details will facilitate the consecration.

Bring into this space one or two decorative items that you *absolutely love*. It's all the better if they are items that have meaning with regard to the story you'll create or your own creativity. These may change over the course of your work, and that is perfectly fine.

You may want to include an altar within your sacred space for your items and making offerings. This can be as simple or elaborate as you choose. A windowsill, a small shelf, or a tabletop are some options. I sometimes use a decorative tray that I can easily move so that I can clean and prepare and replenish offerings in the kitchen and then move it to my sacred space each time I want to make an offering. I will discuss offerings and altars in more detail in chapter 3. For now, just be aware that as you clean and arrange your sacred space, you may wish to set aside a part of it for your altar.

Overall, create a space as pleasing to your eye as you can. Make sure that your journal and pen are handy at all times. If you keep this space sacred, clean, and beautiful, it will serve several purposes. First, it will always be a pleasure for you to enter this space, making for a frame of mind conducive to forming new and positive habits. It will also encourage you to continue your practice. And each time that you come to this sacred space, you will reinforce and build upon your personal understanding of your project. Your mind will begin to associate this space with the work at hand and will trigger the ritual automatically over time as you continue to use this tool.

MINDFULNESS AND YOUR SACRED SENSES

It is valuable to incorporate something for *all* the senses to immerse yourself in your Storytelling Alchemy. You've pleased the eye with the creation of your beautiful sacred space. Now let's think about the other senses.

Bring in a candle, incense, or a fragrance diffuser of some kind to create a pleasing aroma. Plan on using the same scent each time you perform meditations and rituals throughout your Storytelling Alchemy journey to help you move from the mundane to the magickal. Now listen to the space. Your home may already have some built-in sound you find pleasing. But if not, be sure to incorporate a pretty sound. I once lived in an apartment perched just above a major highway. At night, when I closed my eyes, I convinced myself that the sound of the cars going by was really the sound of ocean waves, and it lulled me to sleep beautifully.

Another time, when my young daughter and I were traveling, we stayed a couple of nights in a budget hotel room situated directly above the laundry facilities. There was a vent fan just beneath our window emitting a steady chirping squeak. At first, we had trouble sleeping, and then I told my little girl, "Close your eyes. It's the sound of crickets!" And off to dreamland we went.

So, if you have a built-in sound to work with, consider trying to frame it in some attractive manner. Or, you could add a small water fountain or some soothing music or nature sounds. It should be something you enjoy. If you do choose music, keep to instrumentals, as lyrics can sometimes be distracting.

And so we come to the sense of touch. Pay attention to the temperature of your space and the movement of air. You may want to incorporate a fan if you enjoy the feeling of a breeze against your skin, or you may wish to eliminate that by closing down an A/C vent if that's not something you find pleasing. Be sure that your chair is comfortable, and wear comfortable clothing each time you perform the rituals.

So, what's left, taste? This one is optional. But if you'd like, add something like a small bite of chocolate or fruit or a sip of your favorite tea just before you settle into your process. This should be the same flavor every time to trigger a ritual atmosphere, so be sure it's something you love.

Why are we putting all this focus on the senses before we even begin our exercise? Our senses are the key to becoming mindful in the present moment. In our busy, multitasking lives we are generally focused on getting to some point in the future (or planning for that in some way), or we are thinking about the things that have happened or conversations we've had, and so on. Our minds are constantly trying to remember the grocery list or figure out our schedules. In order to pull our minds off of these concerns and into the present moment, we need to focus on the senses. What is happening *right now*? I'd like you to perform the following brief awareness exercise as soon as you finish reading through it—wherever you are, whatever is going on now. This will help you understand why our senses are so important to the larger practice of meditation.

MINDFULNESS EXERCISE

First, close your eyes and take a deep breath and relax. Get comfortable in your seat. Take a few deep, slow breaths, focusing your attention on the air as it enters your lungs and flows out again. Now, keeping your eyes closed, notice the feeling of the air on your skin, the feeling of your clothes where they touch your body, the feeling of your seat in the chair. Become aware of the temperature of the room. Take in all of the touch sensations that you can notice. Take another deep, slow breath.

Now, notice whether there are any scents in the air. Pay attention to the scent of cooking, perfume, smoke, animals—whatever aromas you are able to perceive. Take notice and be aware of them. Continue to breathe normally.

Now, open your ears and listen. Can you hear voices around you, perhaps distant? Is there music playing anywhere nearby? Can you hear the sounds of weather outside or cars passing? Linger in your listening for a few moments and see if your ability to hear sounds expands.

Finally, open your eyes and pay attention to the colors, shapes, movement, and light around you. Take note of any increased awareness of the view that has resulted from this attention.

This is awareness. This is true presence. When you are in this state, you are operating at what is known as peak performance. This technique is taught to law enforcement and military personnel and employed by martial arts masters. Focusing your awareness on the present moment before meeting any challenge improves the outcome. Your awareness and presence with all your senses give you the ability to respond to stimuli, rather than just reacting. You are simply present and ready for whatever occurs.

During this brief awareness exercise, were you focused on what to buy or cook for dinner this week? Were you thinking about the conversations you've had lately or anything from your past? Or were you present in the moment? This is the power of the senses. Becoming mindful in this way tends to shut down that constant chatter that exists in our heads most of the time. It is freeing, relaxing, and can trigger profound insights and wisdom. And this is why I incorporate the senses as the sixth tool in our tool kit.

Making a habit of mindfulness and presence will progressively improve your focus and mental clarity. These are magickal ingredients. When your personal Will is focused with pinpoint accuracy, your spellcraft powers up.

Before you begin any of the rituals or exercises in this book, I want you to consciously become fully present and mindful each time. This will facilitate the meditative state.

In addition, when you bring all of the senses into a ritual practice in a pleasing way, you'll be more inclined to do it. It's meant to encourage you to make time for yourself and incorporate a healthy habit into your life. It is my hope—and my ulterior motive—to get you hooked on all kinds of meditation, because I believe that presence and mindfulness will save the world. You're welcome!

Also, if you repeat the same sense-stimulating actions each time you perform the rituals, your brain will become entrained to recognize the ritualistic actions, sights, smells, sounds, feelings, and tastes as triggers for the mental state you are about to enter. The ritual will make the practice progressively easier, more natural, and more rewarding.

DREAMS

I would suggest that you also pay close attention to your nighttime dreams throughout this process. During your practice of Storytelling Alchemy, you will be engaging in deep reflection, which will often spark some scenarios that your subconscious will want to play out. In your dreams, you may find some clues from your unconscious or even some inspiration for the story that you will ultimately write.

Since dreams can be like fairytales in their freedom from the constraints of logic and reality, you may experience some interesting insights in your nightly adventures. Keep your journal by your bedside when you sleep, and on waking, record any dreams that you can recall. In the moment of waking, you may not understand if they have significance to your endeavor, but your dreams will reveal things to you and you'll be grateful that you've recorded them.

I teach a workshop called Transformational Storytelling at a wonderful nonprofit called Fresh Start Women's Organization in Phoenix, Arizona. It is a class that incorporates some of the ideas I'm sharing in this book. I encourage my students to use inspirations from their dreams in creating their fairytales.

Some of the women who come to Fresh Start are battling lifetimes of oppression. Some have been raised in cultures that see abuse of women as normal and discourage women from speaking their minds. Many of these women struggle to overcome their previous mind-set of fear and replace it with empowerment. During the workshop, these women would sometimes recall dreams that held significance for their journey and inspired their work on their fairytales.

One woman dreamed of having some obstruction in her throat. In the dream, this was keeping her from speaking and even from breathing. Her fairytale had her pulling this long snakelike obstruction out of her throat, hand over hand, and thus freeing herself to speak and express what was inside her. In her fairytale, she became her own hero.

You may have a dream of being pursued or threatened by some scary monster. Perhaps this monster represents a person from your past who abused you. If so, that image can be incorporated into a fairytale where you are able to slay the monster, forever vanquishing the fear that you will be abused again and empowering you to move forward with confidence.

This is the kind of power that your dreams can have in this endeavor. So, do your best to write them down. You'll be happy that you did.

Many people have trouble recalling their dreams, so here are some tips for increasing your ability to recall and record your dreams.

Affirmations can be very powerful. As I've explained, what we tell ourselves can have a great deal of power in our lives. So each night as you are falling asleep, tell yourself that you will remember your dreams. Do a brief mindfulness exercise. Be sure to remember that your Storytelling Alchemy journal and pen are right at your bedside within easy reach. In fact, as you lie in bed, reach over to your journal and touch it. This will help your body to remember to do that upon waking. Then, simply implant the suggestion to your own mind that when you wake up you will remember the details of your dreams and write them down. You will be surprised at how well this works.

If you wake up in the middle of the night after a dream, reach for your journal and write down whatever impressions you have, even if they are just words. You may write "fear," "ocean," "field," or a person's name. Put down what you can and then leave it.

When you wake in the morning, take it slow. Don't jump out of bed right away if you can avoid it. Take a deep breath, stretch, and just think for a few moments about whatever you can remember and then write down as much as you can.

The act of writing whatever you *can* remember the moment you wake up will, over time, increase how much you recall overall.

There have also been studies done suggesting that B complex vitamins can be helpful for dream recall. Just make sure that you are getting a healthy amount of sleep and nutrition, and you will find the practice increasing.

Now, dream interpretation is a vast subject and has been studied by masters of psychology, magick, and philosophy who are far better at it than I. I do have experience with interpretation, but I find that it is largely intuitive and very personal. I cannot tell you that if you dream of a turtle it represents foundational concepts and benevolence and the support of this earth and all of its spirits, as it does for me. You may have a past in which you were bitten by a snapping turtle, in which case that image will bring up entirely different associations for you.

You can look into some books about dream interpretation, but I've not found them to be very helpful, especially the ones that work like an index where you look up *eagle* and see what the author's interpretation of that is.

I am fond of the philosophies put forth by the psychologist Carl Jung as far as trying to understand your own dreams. If you have months of time to study and understand the complexities of that system, it's a fascinating subject.

But in a nutshell, Jung put forth the idea that in most of our dreams there are images of archetypes. This may be a useful tool to you in your interpretations and we will discuss archetypes a little further in later chapters. If your dream includes, for example, a mother figure or father figure, that may not mean anything about the specific person portrayed in the dream. Instead it may have more to do with your ideas about "Motherhood" or "Fatherhood." Jung is one of many psychologists who affirm that each character, idea, and state in a dream is an aspect of ourselves and not necessarily representative of the actual person or thing portrayed. In other words, if your best friend shows up in your dream, it is more likely a depiction of yourself in your aspect as your own best friend.

I do find that it is a good practice to break down the components of the dream and perhaps try to determine what each piece means to you.

For example, I once had a very significant dream that took place at a dilapidated old train station. Possibly, it was even a postapocalyptic train station. Generally, a train station is a place of travel, a scene of arrivals and departures. But the tracks at this station were no longer in service. So, this could represent some stagnation in my life at the time. In some way, I was stuck.

Be analytical, but trust yourself. Please don't underestimate your innate ability to understand what your own psyche is trying to show you in your dreams.

Record them in your journal and review them throughout your journey. They may reveal more than you think if you give them time.

So now you have your seven essential tools:

1. The mind-set that everything you experience becomes part of the Story You Tell Yourself and understanding how it can change

2. Your Storytelling Alchemy journal and pen

3. Meditation

4. Ritual

5. Your sacred space

6. Your sacred senses

7. Your dreams

Please try to incorporate all of these tools into the work that lies ahead. The preparation is as important as the creative process itself. Do these things for yourself, and you will find this journey very rewarding.

In the next chapter, we'll be talking all about you. Your story is the focus of this book, and we will delve rather deeply. Fear not: I've put some safeguards in place for you. Let's travel on to the next step of this journey.

CHAPTER 3

YOUR STORY—YOUR SPELL

And now it's time to look within. In this chapter, I will help you to examine your past and begin to choose which SYTY you'd like to turn into Your Fairytale. The techniques you will learn in this chapter will help you to remove the emotional charge from your story and collect the facts.

You will be challenged to step back from your opinions about the injustice, wrongdoing, or harmful intentions of others and simply state what happened objectively, so that you can begin to piece together a tale that encompasses all sides with room for compassion for all of its characters and sets the stage for forgiveness.

But while the ultimate goal is to gain a little emotional distance, the process for choosing which SYTY you want to work with requires some reflection. It is necessary to feel the pain first and realize you are ready to be done with it before you begin writing or creating. But do try to remember that you are reviewing these memories, not reliving them.

Start to think about a story or stories you'd like to change or let go. Pay attention to your history and seek out the parts that bring you pain, sadness, anger, resentment, and shame. Those are the places to look for the most profound and meaningful transformations.

The poet Wallace Stevens said, "The intolerable image is the transformational image."

To me, this is saying that the thing that you find the most difficult to look at is the thing that can bring you the deepest change and the most profound understanding. And in my experience, this is true.

Make a list in your journal of the possible stories or hurts that you may want to work with. Here are some ideas about where to look in your emotions and your history.

If there is an encounter that you sometimes relive in your mind, perhaps where you argue better than you did during the actual event or where you still feel the same anger or sadness upon reflecting as you did while it was happening, that's a good place to begin.

If there was a grief or loss that you've had to face in the past which is still limiting you now, explore that.

Perhaps you are dealing with something challenging and painful currently in your life. Current events are fair game for Storytelling Alchemy! In fact, writing a successful or triumphant outcome before the real-life details unfold can have a very positive effect on the actual situation. The story is a spell that helps bring the desired outcome into being.

By the way, stories from your past that bring up happy and joyful emotions are not good candidates for transformation. You may turn them into fairytales, if you wish, just for fun, but happy memories are empowering and should be kept that way!

Another way to draw out the story that you may want to work with is to look at the situations in your life today that you are not happy with. You may not think that there is a story about these situations because you don't know why they exist in your life right now, but looking closer may uncover a root cause buried in your past. For example, if you struggle with your weight or have body image issues, you may want to explore the feelings behind that. If you are struggling to get a business off the ground, but have issues around money, spend some time trying to think of possible reasons why that's the case.

These kinds of "story starters" are almost always based in the damaging emotion we call shame. Anything about which you feel shameful is a good candidate for Your Fairytale.

Remember that the blocks that impede our progress are quite often unconscious, so you may not be able to discover the reasons for these things just by thinking about them. But don't let that stop you from picking one of these ideas to work with. The process that we go through in this book and the process of writing may bring some unconscious beliefs to consciousness so that they can be dealt with.

Let's get started on the path to figure out which SYTY you will work on by learning about the ritual offerings that will trigger a meditative mood and emotional distance from your stories and then a memory meditation for reviewing the stories that you want to bring into the light.

RITUAL OFFERINGS

Now that you've created your sacred space and you have your journal at the ready to record important information, it's time to learn about ritual offerings. These are not elaborate and they needn't take much time, but I encourage you to be consistent and perform the offering each time you return to your Storytelling Alchemy practice—before each meditation and before each session of creating.

An offering is like a prayer. It is an acknowledgment of Spirit and perhaps even gratitude before the favor. What we want to accomplish with an offering is to establish a relationship with whatever spirits or powers-that-be may be present, in the hopes that they will help us in our endeavors. You are offering them your attention and some physical object or action that will, presumably, please them in an effort to open the pathways of communication in a way that will be beneficial. This sort of offering is just like lighting a candle in church.

Choose a small area within your sacred space where your offerings will take place. This will serve as your altar. As I said earlier, your space may be a table or shelf, a windowsill, or a tray that you can carry for easy cleaning and replenishment of the offerings. Whichever you choose, remember that this is a dedicated space for that purpose. Always pay attention to its condition and keep it clean and tidy. As we discuss how and to whom the offerings are made, you may find that there are certain items you will always want to keep on your altar. These items can be symbolic images representing the spirit you've chosen to work with or they could be as simple as a candle or an incense holder. But do try to keep your sacred space uncluttered and pleasing to the eye.

Now, let's work out exactly to whom or what this offering is being given. Following is a list of some spiritual and/or psychological entities that may aid you in your work. This is not meant to be a complete or exhaustive list of the types of spirits that exist; I've just included some of those that might be helpful in your practice of Storytelling Alchemy. You may choose one or all or any combination that makes sense to your endeavor.

Deity: God, Yahweh, Jesus, Allah, Athena, Odin, Diana, Zeus, and so many others

Whatever *you* call a deity may be incorporated into this practice. Personally, I make daily offerings to Athena. In my spiritual life, she is my patron goddess. I've yet to decide for myself whether she is an actual "living" entity that has life and Will outside of the human-created mythological idea of her or whether she is a psychological construct that helps me to focus my own inner wisdom in a way that is consistent with her mythology and with my desired outcomes. In the end, I don't think it matters because the result is the same. The act of making an offering puts the image in my mind of a powerful entity who can help me. Specifically for me, Athena's weaving abilities translate well to writing as "the weaving of a tale." And invoking her energies of wisdom and creativity helps me feel that I have support for the act of writing.

And, in keeping with our discussion of the interconnectedness of all things, I do believe that deities that are known, worshipped, acknowledged, prayed to, and written about repeatedly take on the energy of the thoughts of those people who have prayed and worshipped, and the spirits then become even more powerful through that.

If you choose to make offerings to a deity, make it one you are familiar with already *or* do some research into their stories to help you decide whether this one spirit or another can assist you in your task.

Land Spirits: Fairies, local legends, spirits with significance for the indigenous peoples of the area where you live, animal spirits or totems, etc.

This list could be quite long. Again, it's up to you. You may know of something fitting or you may decide to do some research into the area where you live and its history to find something that suits your journey. I tend to make offerings to the general idea of "land spirits" so as to capture whatever energies may be present. It is simply a good-faith offering to say, "I know you exist, even though I may not know you individually at this time, but I offer you this gift so that, if you are so inclined, you may help me accomplish my goal."

Ancestors/Beloved Dead

Yes, I'm sort of talking about ghosts here. Many people ascribe to the idea that those who have gone before us have power in the here and now. Recent studies have shown that our very DNA may hold wisdom and knowledge of our ancestors. Making an offering to the beloved dead may be an especially good idea if Your Fairytale includes stories that involve family members, whether they are still living or have passed on. An offering generally honoring your ancestors and beloved dead will focus your mind on the collective will of a family line that, no doubt, embraces honor, goodness, peace, forgiveness, and enlightenment. That is why family lines endure. Regardless of your personal family history, your ancestors *must* have desired the evolvement of their line. And that means that they will be willing to be on your side in your endeavor to become the best version of yourself.

Your Own Creativity/Genius

First, let's look at the words *inspired* and *inspiration*. These words, literally translated, mean "infused with spirit." In ancient Rome the word *genius* referred to a specific spirit or entity that was assigned to an individual, which bestowed inspiration upon that human for his or her creative endeavors. Today, we see the word *genius* as something a person *is*, rather than something a person *has*. It may seem a minute distinction, but it can be very helpful in the creative process to imagine that there is an entity that provides one with the talent, the transformative ideas, the "genius" to bring about the birth of a project. In fact, the origins of the word *genius* are related to the Greek word for birth. The creative process brings something new into the world. That is a gestation and birthing process. Allow yourself to imagine that there may be a benevolent entity outside of yourself invested in the birthing of Your Fairytale.

I have a Navajo storyteller figurine. I call her Alvarita, which means "truth-teller." She sits on an altar of mine, and whenever I sit down to write, I invite her to join. I make an offering to her and ask her to help me be true in my endeavor and to act as my creative "genius" so that whatever I may write, it will be of some value to someone. You may find a symbol of your genius as well. But, even if you don't, think about making an offering to whatever genius may be available to you in your endeavor to create Your Fairytale.

What to Offer

This is up to you, but consider the mythology, legend, or idea of the spirit to which the offering is being made. Offerings should correlate to the spirit you envision, to their mythology if that applies, to your feelings about an entity, to its known history. Lighting a candle is appropriate and so is burning incense. Sometimes an offering can be a sacrifice of your time and consideration, perhaps a simple prayer or the writing of a poem.

Offerings that I make to Athena include olive oil and olives because, according to her mythology, the olive tree is sacred to her. But there are many deities whose mythologies suggest that they would like a certain type of food or beverage. Do some research and

STORYTELLING ALCHEMY

then guess what they may like. If the offering is approached with sincerity and a willing spirit, the deity will either accept willingly or instruct you regarding its desires.

Once I kept an altar dedicated to the planetary deity Venus for a spell that I was performing. At the times when I made offerings and sat quietly meditating on my gratitude for my expected outcome, I would become aware of certain energies, words, objects. Some of these awarenesses were instructions. For a few days in a row, I brought her flowers, sweets, and pretty stones. One day, I asked her if she was pleased with the offerings, and immediately in my mind's eye I saw the altar in a different location in my home adorned with two specific items in my possession: a green silk scarf and a beautiful art glass piece. I followed the instructions and relocated her altar and added to it those things she had shown me. The outcome was a raging success. So remember that listening and paying attention to your impressions while making offerings is an important part of this practice. The clues can be rather subtle. Don't overthink it, and just be open to considering alternatives and doing the best you can.

Offerings that I make to the land spirits are generally incense that I am aware the indigenous peoples of this land have used for hundreds of years in their own spiritual practices. I've also used offerings that I'm aware will be taken by the animals that live in my area. For a time, I offered bits of bread or crackers to the birds that frequent my location. It is my understanding that the natural inhabitants of your area are embodiments and representations of the land spirits, just as we are embodiments and representations of the deities we revere.

I give fresh, purified water to my own creative genius. This is a life-sustaining element, and I want my creative genius to live on and thrive. Open yourself to the genius that lives and exists to help you birth your creativity. Perhaps your genius requires red wine or shortbread or steak. Allow your own intuition to guide you in this practice.

At this point, many people ask what to do with "leftovers" of the physical offerings afterward. Again, I will encourage you to use your own intuition in this regard. If your offering was something edible which is perishable, it's perfectly okay to just dispose of it however you see fit. If you offered water, feel free to use it to water houseplants.

Some people bury the remains of their offerings; others advocate dropping the remains in a flowing and moving body of water such as a river or stream. If you choose to use either of these methods, please refrain from doing so with any nonbiodegradable or inorganic items.

If the offerings were nonperishable food items, such as candies or alcohol or dried fruit, feel free to consume them yourself! Whatever you choose to do here, know that the way you dispose of the past offering will never be wrong in any way that would cancel out the intention of the offering itself. The point is to use common sense and allow yourself to be guided by your own inner wisdom.

MEDITATION

Now that you have an understanding of what should be done at the beginning of each exercise, let's move on to the practice of meditation.

We've discussed the many life experiences that you may choose to transform into Your Fairytale. Over the next couple of weeks, I want you to perform what I call a Memory Meditation several times. Choose one of the life experiences that you have been mulling over for Your Fairytale to explore for each Memory Meditation session that you plan. Follow the instructions below. And remember to review, not relive, these experiences.

MEMORY MEDITATION EXERCISE

First, make your offering. Perhaps this involves the lighting of a candle or incense. Perhaps it is a spoken prayer. Remember what you've decided to do, and perform that ritual now.

Each time you begin this exercise, take a moment to become aware of, acknowledge, and give gratitude for the pleasing experience of the moment. As you approach your sacred, creative space, take in the beauty, the order, and the overall aesthetic and appreciate what you've created. Allow yourself to feel gratitude—and pride!

As you settle into your chair, acknowledge the comfort. Notice the feeling of the air on your skin. Close your eyes for a moment and give those sensations their due.

Then light your candle or incense or start your fragrance diffuser and take in the scent deeply. Appreciate that small pleasure.

Turn your awareness to the sound. Start your music or nature sounds and just take a few brief seconds to listen closely and be thankful for the beauty of the sound.

Now, if you've chosen to incorporate the sense of taste, take that bite or that sip and give it your full attention. Enjoy it deeply.

And give thanks in this present moment *for* this present moment. Recognize that this present moment is filled with pleasurable experience that you've created for yourself.

Take a deep breath, close your eyes, rest, and relax into your chair. If you feel some tension or discomfort, move around and stretch your muscles, and when you feel right, settle back into a relaxed position in your chair. Continue to breathe evenly.

As you relax and continue to breathe comfortably, understand that you exist in this safe, beautiful, sensual atmosphere for which you are grateful. You will always begin and end your sessions here, surrounded by this world of sensual pleasure that you have chosen to create.

Continue to breathe, enjoy, and be grateful.

In any meditation practice, it can be helpful to tune into your own body. Place your hand over your heart, become still, and listen and feel for your own heartbeat. As you begin to perceive its rhythm, inhale to the count of five heartbeats, pause for two heartbeats, exhale for five heartbeats, and pause again for two heartbeats at the bottom of your exhale. You may find your heartbeat slowing, and that is fine. Repeat this extended breath five times. Then lower your hand to your lap and continue to breathe normally.

When you feel peaceful, relaxed, and ready, allow your mind to wander to that time in your past when you felt betrayed or harmed or challenged in some way.

But step back from that scene: Observe it, as if you were a fly on the wall. Try to eliminate judgment about what is happening. Float above the scenes and simply remember and view the action as it unfolds before you.

Remember that you are not being harmed anew. You are seated in your sacred space amid its beauty, and you are safe. If you start to feel otherwise at any time during this exercise, return your attention to the safety of your sacred space and try again at another time.

Simply observe the action of your memory. Listen to the words that were spoken. Remember as clearly as you can and without judgment of good, bad, happy, sad, etc. Simply see.

Allow the images to play out like a film.

When you feel as though the scene has reached its conclusion—or come to a place you feel is a natural break—breathe deeply and remember your impressions.

Allow yourself to recall that you are, actually, in your sacred creative space, enjoying all these lovely sensations.

Rest in that for a moment. Then, when you feel ready, open your eyes and return to alertness.

Immediately write down your impressions of the memory in your journal. Be sure to record any new insights that you've gained from observing it objectively. Write this log in the third person by referring to all the characters as he/she, including—and maybe especially—yourself.

This will help you begin to see the memory as a story instead of the SYTY.

For a week or two, try to perform as many offering rituals and memory meditations as you can. Each time, you will appreciate your sacred space, make your offerings, and choose a different story from your past to contemplate.

Recording details will help you remember which stories pique the deepest emotions in you. But don't decide which one you want to use for Your Fairytale just yet. Simply allow yourself to be with these stories and the emotions they bring for the time being.

Grounding

You may discover that you are left with some unpleasant feelings or simply an energy that seems uncomfortable after these sessions. Grounding is useful to dispel these feelings.

Grounding is a means that allows a person to reconnect with the here and now and dispel any energy or negative emotion that may have accumulated or that may seem to stagnate in the body and mind. This process involves, as the name implies, connecting to the earth in some way.

You can visualize a root attached to your body and entering the ground. See the excess energy or negative emotion leaving your body through this root and entering the earth. It is said that the earth has the ability to neutralize these energies so they no longer have a connotation of "bad" or "good." Upon entering the earth, they simply become energy to be utilized in whatever way is necessary.

You may prefer to actually go outside and put your hands on a tree, which already has roots entering the ground. This may make it easier to do the visualization.

While going through this process, you may also absorb some positive energy from the tree or the earth.

Some people find that eating something is very grounding. It allows your mind to focus once again on your body and the mundane functions of life on earth, bringing you back into the present moment. Having a bit of bread, which is of the earth, can dispel your excess energies and emotions.

Some people feel that simply bending down and touching the ground is a useful way of grounding.

Use whatever method works for you. Just remember that you don't have to carry those negative emotions from the past around with you. If you can find a way to dispel them, do so.

Recall

If you have trouble recalling the events of the memories you have chosen, try to think about the emotions and the sensations relating to those five senses we've discussed. Sensations can frequently trigger a memory. The sensation of entering the ocean for a swim will frequently remind me of a time when I was a small child and afraid of the waves. My father picked me up and threw me in. I tumbled and scraped against the bottom of sand and shells and struggled to turn and reach the surface and air.

There may be a physical sensation or a certain smell or visual stimulus that will put you in mind of the memory you are trying to reach. If it's possible, allow yourself to experience that sensation. If you remember smelling a pie baking in the oven during an altercation with your family that is the subject of your memory, try to reproduce that scent to aid in your recall.

In this endeavor, of course, stop short of reproducing the scent of a raging fire or some other harmful event. In such a case, use your memory of the scent or sensation instead to spark the rest of the scene.

If you are having trouble remembering specifics, reaching into the senses to help you remember may be a useful tool for moving forward through the exercise.

You may also wish to incorporate some exercises that will help boost your memory in general. You can search for some that make sense to you, but as an example you can try drawing a map of a location that you've recently visited or practice memorizing a grocery or to-do list and see how accurate you can be. There are many ways to improve the memory. In this sense, the brain works like a muscle. The more you "work out" the memory muscle, the better you'll be at memory in general.

Another useful thing to do when you simply can't remember something is to just get up and take up something else for a while. Take a walk, do some exercise, wash the dishes. Have you ever noticed if you look up at the night sky you can sort of see a bright star in your peripheral vision, but when you turn your eyes to look directly at it, it disappears? Avert your direct gaze and it appears bright again. Sometimes I think memories are like this. They get brighter when you're not focused directly on them. So, if you feel really stuck, take a walk and see if that helps.

Benefits of Storytelling Alchemy

During these days as you reflect, you are deliberately choosing to feel sadness and hurt. You may tend to want to stop and discontinue your reflection if it becomes too painful. It's a good idea at the same time to consider the benefits you will reap from rewriting/re-creating the SYTY in this way at the end of each session. So let's look at some of those you can expect as you move forward with this practice.

Holding Space

You've likely heard of the concept of "holding space," but what does that really mean?

When you share any of your challenging experiences with a friend or loved one, the response—assuming this person cares for you and wants to be supportive—probably includes expressions of concern, exclamations of injustice, encouragements to ignore this or to somehow change the way you feel about it all. People find it uncomfortable to sit with their own emotions, let alone the unpleasant emotions of someone else, so they will try to "fix" your problem or convince you that "it was all for the best" or to "take this as a learning experience." And while those things may all be true, what is really needed when you first share a difficult life experience is simple, nonjudging, active, spacious listening.

When we share our difficulty or vulnerability or tragedy, we need a space that "allows." I'm referring to the person who listens and can stay still and accepting of whatever your feelings may be. They don't try to change anything or try to convince you of how you *should* feel. They simply allow you to tell your tale acting as an open and attentive witness. Such people are very rare. But this practice of listening with mindfulness and presence and allowing is extremely healing.

And now that you've had a little bit of experience with meditation and the sacred practice of making offerings and creating sacred space, you are beginning to get the idea of what "holding space" really means. The process of Storytelling Alchemy will allow *you* to be the one who "holds space" for your story and to reap the healing benefits of that.

As an added bonus, it can turn you into one of those remarkable people who are able to truly listen and be present, and that is a gift to the world.

Perspective

The work of transforming the SYTY into Your Fairytale will bring you some much-needed perspective. When we tell ourselves our story, we already know the background. We already have opinions about all the characters and events. We already have a context.

But in having to write down a coherent plotline with a beginning, middle, and end, we are forced to look at it from different angles. Will it make sense to someone who doesn't have any knowledge of the history behind it? How will you develop the characters and their personalities?

You will have to examine the chronology as well. In real life, events are often unfolding with different people simultaneously.

Sometimes, the story is better if the events are told in a different order than they happened.

All of this puts you in the position of the outsider looking in. You will undoubtedly discover aspects of the story that you've never considered before.

Objectivity

Precisely because you are required to step back in order to tell the tale in a way that someone would want to read it, you also have to ask questions about the motivations of all the characters. You'll be asked to examine and understand the actions of each one, including yourself, in a way that can be put down on paper and comprehended by an outside reader. This removes—or at least lessens—the tendency to take only one side.

When looking at the SYTY in this way, you will be able to see the bigger picture and give a little more compassion to the characters and foster a little more understanding of its events.

Which brings us to . . .

Compassion

In order to be a good story, each decision maker, each character, each player must be given a depth that the reader will appreciate. This doesn't mean one character didn't act inappropriately or another character wasn't wrong within the situation; it just means that readers need to understand their motivations.

This practice can help you develop compassion for the other participants in your memory. And if the story you've chosen happens to include your own shame or guilt, then it's even more important to develop that compassion for yourself as a character.

Self-Examination

Socrates said that the unexamined life is not worth living. Examining our own motivations, actions, and feelings is wholly valuable in every instance and can add depth to life. Storytelling Alchemy is a great—and sometimes even fun, I swear!—way to study your own behaviors, habits, and reactions.

You may discover—or uncover—a deeply held belief that, once conscious, can be easily proven false. I'll be sharing a perfect example of this from my own life in a later chapter. You may realize that you have a pattern of behavior that sabotages your relationships and begin to make changes. You may discover a habit of perceiving hurt where there is none intended.

These are very powerful realizations and can lead to lasting change and fulfillment in your life.

Understanding and Forgiveness

> How does one know if she has forgiven? You tend to feel sorrow over the circumstance instead of rage, you tend to feel sorry for the person rather than angry with him. You tend to have nothing left to say about it all.
> —Clarissa Pinkola Estes

In the aftermath of all of this objective, compassionate perspective while writing, you will likely be able to reach a point of forgiveness. Your exploration and deep examination of yourself and the other players in Your Fairytale will enable you to heal old hurts and let go of resentments. And that is an exquisite freedom. That is removal of a great scar. Forgiveness is healing, and healing is the beginning of something new and better.

Helping Others

Your Fairytale will help others. You won't have to publish a book like I have or teach classes or become a public speaker on the subject of healing to share the benefits of this process with others. The truth is so much simpler than that.

The story you write—whatever it is and whatever it's about—will be helpful to anyone who reads it or hears it. This is a promise I make to you. If you put your real and true emotions into Your Fairytale and if you share it with those you love—or anyone you wish to—people will benefit from it. They will be somehow enlightened, drawn closer to you, or have some of their own feelings and false beliefs revealed to them. Remember that once you've written it, your story will be a catalyst for healing however you choose to share it.

Magick!

If you haven't previously delved into the value of practicing magick regularly, the instructions and exercises taught in this book will give you a foundation for doing so. I mentioned before that meditation has been a profound catalyst for change and improvement of my life—and that's true—but the practice of magick has given me the power to create outcomes I never could have hoped for in the past. If meditation is the brain, magick is the muscle. You will be able to take your newfound focus and power up your spellcraft to create the life you've always wanted. I realize as I write this that it sounds like hype. It's not. Wait and see. Together we'll embark on this journey, and I will help you learn how to get the results you wish for.

The experience I've had with the practice of Storytelling Alchemy has brought gifts that I never expected or imagined. I've gained a confidence and freedom I didn't believe possible. And I've brought to the surface many unconscious beliefs that previously limited me so that I could make lasting and satisfying changes in my life.

Remember, dear reader—dear *adventurer*—while you are reflecting on your pain, that this kind of outcome is possible for you. Expect these benefits. Look forward to your freedom. This will help you get through the difficult parts of the process to the good stuff. Soldier on, my friend. It's not easy; it's just worth it.

Now let's take a closer look at storytelling in general. I believe you will be helped in your journey by understanding the meaning, significance, and importance of storytelling in human history.

CHAPTER 4

STORYTELLING: EVOLUTION, CULTURAL LEGACIES, AND MAGICKAL PURPOSES

So what, exactly, is a story? We'll begin with the basics. In its simplest sense, a story is the iteration of events unfolding in time. Stories have a beginning, a middle, and an end. The telling involves characters (the players and their roles), setting (the location and situation in which the events unfold), and plot (the sequence and purpose of the unfolding events). Let's look at a little bit of the history of storytelling in general. Then we can explore the human needs that sparked the practice of storytelling, as well as some examples, and discuss the magick of story as well as how it can shape lives, events, cultures, and even human evolution itself.

THE ORIGINS OF STORYTELLING

Storytelling goes back long before written language. Oral traditions exist in every culture around the world, and stories have been handed down from generation to generation for thousands—maybe even hundreds of thousands—of years. In oral traditions, stories tend to change and evolve over time. The speaker of the tale will embellish, edit, and add a bit of personal flair. Just like in a game of "telephone," the story changes a little with each telling. Many of the oldest written stories are the result of hundreds of retellings of verbal stories, finally made static by the act of writing them down.

In many Native American oral traditions, there exists the Spider Woman or Spider Grandmother. In some traditions, she is a creation deity; in others, she is the keeper of history, the storyteller. In yet others, she is credited with teaching the people how to spin thread and weave so that they would no longer have to rely on animal skins for clothing.

In ancient China, there is a myth of the Candle Dragon, a vast creature with such light in its eyes that when it blinked, night fell. The myths go on to describe how the seasons were connected to the breathing of the beast and that the candle it held in its mouth was meant to light the way for humans to find paradise after death. The written texts of this story date back as far as 500 BCE, with the oral tradition reaching much further back into China's history.

The Mahabharata, an epic story from India, is the longest poem we know of. It is a tale of war and battle, but also includes spiritual teachings. The Bhagavad Gita, a 700-verse story contained within the Mahabharata, features a famous battle scene. Bhagavad Gita can be interpreted as meaning "Song of the Lord" and includes what many scholars hold to be a comprehensive distillation of Hindu beliefs. The text of the Mahabharata was first written down around 400 BCE; however, evidence suggests the original tale may have begun to be told as much as 500 years earlier.

The oldest written story to have been discovered currently is the ancient Mesopotamian epic Gilgamesh, which dates back over three thousand years.

Meanwhile, the stories of Australia's Aborigine people have been shown to be some of the oldest known. The tales they tell include descriptions of a time before the Great Barrier Reef existed when that region was dry land. Geologists have confirmed that this was indeed the case at one time in the history of that continent. This corroboration indicates that those stories may have originated up to 13,000 years ago.

These ancient tales are only the ones that have survived and been documented. These are the stories that have been preserved either by continuous oral traditions of surviving cultures or by writing. But storytelling began long before all of these ancient tales. Images on the walls of caves attest to that. Perhaps even before humans discovered ways to engrave or paint those images, and even before any language as we know it came into being, stories would have been told in a kind of pantomime.

Perhaps you can imagine a time when humans were hunter-gatherers living in caves and relying on their skills for survival. There must have been a time when one hunter was able to tell the story of how an animal behaved. He must have been able, at some point, to look at the tracks and signs of that animal and understand the story those signs told and what they meant. He would have understood that the story of the signs could predict where the animal *would be* so that he could more successfully hunt it to feed his family.

It is theorized that these early humans may have been performing rituals where the *story* of a successful hunt was told—and probably even acted out—in advance of their hunt in order to ensure a successful outcome.

In this sense, storytelling became a *genetic characteristic* of humans—a trait of evolution. When any animal develops a characteristic that lends to the successful survival and/or procreation of the species, that trait tends to persist because the less successful members of the species who don't possess it die in greater numbers.

Certainly, when man developed the skill of storytelling—coupled with the magickal practice of retelling the stories with intentions regarding the future outcome—he became a more successful hunter-gatherer, and therefore, this skill occurred more and more frequently in the gene pool, with evolution solidifying our legacy of storytelling. This is evidenced by the fact that storytelling exists everywhere. There is no human community that doesn't tell stories. Storytelling may be the very thing that makes us human.

Anthropologist Sir James George Frazer wrote about such practices of early humanity in his influential book *The Golden Bough: A Study of Magic and Religion*, first published in 1890.

Our ancestors' practice of acting out a successful outcome before a hunt took place is an example of "sympathetic magick." This form of magick relies on correspondence and imitation for its power. Those cave images attest to this practice. And perhaps the ancient humans used bones and skins of previously hunted animals in their ritual to make stronger connections to their desired outcomes.

Frazer wrote that sympathetic magick included two categories of assumptions or laws that the practitioners would have believed in: (i) the Law of Similarity, where two things that are alike can affect one another; and (ii) the Law of Contagion, where two items that were once in physical contact can still affect one another over distances after that physical contact is broken.

If this last bit sounds familiar, you may be recalling the entanglement theory we discussed earlier, where two particles of light that had once been connected were shown to affect one another even when separated by long distances in an experiment performed in Geneva in 1997. The theories that led to that experimentation began to take form around the 1930s.

A book discussing the primitive magickal thinking of prehistoric humans written in 1889 predicted a scientific theory in the 1930s that was proven in 1997. Isn't that interesting and magickal? Is modern science finally coming to prove the "primitive magickal" beliefs held by early humans? Or has all the research and writing about such topics created a world where the belief has become fact?

STORIES ABOUT STORYTELLING

Now, moving forward in time from the cave dwellers, there are myths and stories in each culture *about* storytelling. It has been a revered and important practice in civilizations spanning the globe.

Anansi, the African folktale character, is described as possessing the knowledge of all stories. Tales of this spider-god have persisted and spread from West Africa to the West Indies and the Caribbean and even into the Creole traditions of the southern United States.

Native American storyteller dolls depict a person with open mouth, surrounded by listeners—often children. These figures emphasize oral traditions, where storytelling is used as a teaching tool and a medium for preserving the history and culture of a people. The first clay storyteller figurine was created by Cochiti Pueblo artist Helen Cordero in 1964. As the figures grew in popularity, artists from many other Native American tribes began creating them, incorporating imagery that honored their own tribe's storytelling traditions. There is an example of a small storyteller figurine created by a Navajo artist on page 40. But there are so many beautiful versions, I encourage you to consult that great oracle Google and check out some museum-quality images. Or, better still, visit a museum where you might find one and enjoy the rich, meaningful imagery firsthand.

CULTURAL MEMORY EXERCISE

Remember to approach each exercise in this book in the same way, incorporating the senses, making offerings, and expressing gratitude for the sacred writing space you've created and are currently enjoying.

Are there any stories from your personal heritage that have been passed down to you? What types of stories have been told in your family or in your culture for generations? Spend about twenty to thirty minutes meditating on and writing about the stories that your family and your culture have taught to you. Just explore what you can remember about them. Examine how they made you feel and what you learned from them. Consider whether you feel they are worthy of passing on to the next generation, and why or why not.

What is the purpose of storytelling? Why is it so important to humans?

In his acceptance speech for the Nobel Prize, author John Steinbeck said, "Literature is as old as speech. It grew out of human need for it, and it has not changed except to become more needed."

The reasons for storytelling have changed and evolved since its origins. The first stories, told by cave dwellers, were surely based in necessities. Their stories aided in hunting and gathering and providing shelter, safety, and security. These kinds of stories sustained the very survival of the tellers and listeners. And those who listened well persisted and thrived.

As time went on, stories took on other aspects. When Native American tribes honored the Spider Grandmother spirit in stories told young listeners, they were teaching useful skills, as it was Spider Grandmother who taught her people how to spin and weave fabric. The Candle Dragon of China factors in other stories attempting to explain the cycles and phenomena of nature.

As cultures grew in richness and complexity, their stories became more complex as well. They could be used to teach morality and preserve history, as with the stories of Anansi, the West African spider-god.

For many families, clans, or tribes, a story was a kind of legacy handed down from one generation to the next. These stories educate and comfort the people of a particular understanding. Sometimes, they offer explanations of geographical significance. In other cases, stories preserve custom and culture. The Celt-Iberians believed that speaking the stories of their ancestors and honored dead would keep them alive in a way and preserve the very honor of the family line.

Eventually, myths and spiritual stories developed. Presumably, myths were divinely inspired, and such encounters with the divine produced deep and intricate tales designed to bring the listener or reader to a point of wonder, where a meeting with the divine could occur.

The Sumerian saga of Gilgamesh includes mythology depicting fantastic beasts, gods and goddesses, and tales of superhuman abilities. All of this creates a sense of awe, which may inspire that moment when one is transported outside of one's own earthly existence into the realm of the mystical.

The working of magick often utilizes these kinds of stories to foster the energy that comes from that still point of awe in communion with the divine. A kind of ecstasy is produced. In that moment of awe, the ego and our conscious ideas about exactly who and what we are fade to almost nothing, and we are shown the reality of our vast and omnipotent souls. That is the kind of energy that gets results! That is the still point of creation itself.

These traits in storytelling persist to this day. Mythology has been incorporated into popular fantasy and sci-fi. Stories for pure entertainment are a rather late addition to the mix, but they still take inspiration from the classics. And even as pure entertainment, the story must include some kind of "hook" or emotional connection with the audience in order to be appreciated. Take, for instance, today's popular horror genre, which seems to tend quite often toward the idea of the "living dead." A portion of the epic poem Gilgamesh has the goddess Ishtar threatening to raise the dead so that they would outnumber the living and devour them. So there you have it: the earliest piece of written literature that we know of was, at least in part, a zombie story!

All good stories go beyond mere entertainment, to reach the unconscious part of our minds.

So when you think about it, storytelling is deeply embedded in the human psyche. Its significance cannot be overstated. Our very evolution has relied upon it, and the human spirit has been molded by the best of the stories from our history.

Good stories reach into the soul, teach something of value, give the reader a new insight or catharsis. They can help us understand something about our world or ourselves. This is the kind of storytelling that can change the listener. Stories that reach the heart—in other words, that push through our conscious blocks to the unconscious—have the power to heal and transform. And transformation, dear reader, is alchemy.

FAVORITE STORIES EXERCISE

Sit quietly in your sacred space for a few minutes and recall some of your favorite stories of all time. Don't limit yourself to childhood stories or books you've read. Film is story too, as are plays and TV shows. In reality, any kind of art can tell a story. Just take some time to muse and recall as many stories as you can that have moved you to tears of joy or sadness or made you think. Record the stories you enjoyed and even the ones you've been addicted to. (I confess to binge-watching the popular television series *Supernatural.*) Try to remember as many as you can, and write them all down.

After your list is finished, read through your selections and see if you can find any common thread. Write down your thoughts about this as well. Then make a simple offering of gratitude to the creative genius that brought your favorites into the world.

THE DIFFERENT GENRES OF STORYTELLING

Next, we will take a look at the different genres of story and study a few examples. This brief examination will help you consider what makes up the different types of stories and that will assist you with the actual writing of Your Fairytale. It is my hope that you will also be quite entertained by the stories we explore, so read on!

As we delve into the various types of story, it is my goal to inspire you and spark your imagination. You may discover one type of storytelling that matches up with the events of your life, or you may simply find that one genre is something you enjoy and thus will be more enjoyable to create. Keep an open mind as you peruse these options and begin to think about some examples of these genres that have inspired you in the past.

When it comes to written tales, there are several different classic types, although you'll find many of them intermingle and overlap, and these stories can be engaged with through any sort of medium. Remember that Your Fairytale may take the form of a written story, a film, a work of visual or performance art, or some combination like a graphic novel or comic book. Use whatever medium speaks to you. Your story may be produced entirely with computer graphics. You may wish to write an epic poem or decorate your backyard! The point is, don't limit yourself to just the writing. I'll be discussing the written word type of tale quite a bit, but that is to organize the ideas and the content of Your Fairytale. *You* will ultimately decide how that is expressed. Whatever form Your Fairytale does take, the thoughts and ideas behind it still have to be sorted into some kind of initial order. This exploration of writing will help you do that.

Stories of all kinds quite frequently fall into the format of the Hero's Journey, also known as the monomyth. In general terms, this is the story of an individual who goes on a quest, fights a battle, and, ultimately, wins out and returns transformed. Well-known mythologist Joseph Campbell wrote in his book *The Hero with a Thousand Faces*:

> A hero ventures forth from the world of common day into a region of supernatural wonder: fabulous forces are there encountered and a decisive victory is won: the hero comes back from this mysterious adventure with the power to bestow boons on his fellow man.

I will delve more deeply into the phases of the Hero's Journey in chapter 10 on techniques, which gives you some practical story-writing tips, but for now, allow the idea of the basic components of the Hero's Journey to offer you a framework for some of the genres of story that you know well.

The Hero's Journey can present itself in several different types of adventures. In some, the hero slays the dragon or defeats the monster. *Beowulf* is a classic example of this type.

Others find the protagonist being redeemed or reborn in some way, like Ebenezer Scrooge in the Dickens classic *A Christmas Carol*.

Almost always, the main character—which, in Your Fairytale will, of course, be you—faces some peril or descends into a kind of dark night of the soul that challenges and transforms them. The whole gamut of human emotion is represented in the Hero's Journey: apprehension, fear, courage, curiosity, wonderment, confusion, incredulity, denial, surprise, perseverance, exhaustion, pain, love, hatred, anger, justification, ignorance, triumph, and joy.

These types of stories are desirable because the average person wants to experience all of those things that show up for the hero. And the fact is that we do. It may not be on as grand a scale as the *Odyssey* or *Star Wars*, but the Hero's Journey is happening in all of our lives, all of the time. That's why we identify with those stories and how they touch our hearts. And this is why the SYTY can be transformed.

And this basic format can find its way into many different genres such as fables, myths, legends, folktales, and fairytales.

A fable is usually a short tale that teaches a moral or a truth about life. Often the main characters are animals, which is a technique that makes the story pleasing to children. Let's delve into one as an example.

One of the most famous fables of Aesop is "The Tortoise and the Hare." This story imparts the universal truth that speed is not the only component to "winning" a race and sometimes consistency carries more importance. The slow, methodical, but unrelenting progress of the tortoise wins out over the quick, overconfident bravado of the hare. Or, to quote the simple phrase that everyone can recognize as the moral of this fable, "Slow and steady wins the race."

We can identify with this story line whether we perceive ourselves to be the tortoise or the hare. If we are the person who is constantly running to keep up or the person who is admonished for being methodical, we see something of value here, some overarching truth that makes sense of our world and gives us a reason to think.

FABLES EXERCISE

As always, begin with your awareness meditation and gratitude. Make an offering, if you like. Then try to recall some of the fables from your childhood and write down the ones that had an impact on you when you were young. Did the moral hit home? Or did the story frighten you in some way? Try to remember all of the feelings you had when hearing or reading the story. Write down your impressions in your journal.

A myth generally occurs on a much grander scale and seeks to convey some history, origin story, or explanation for a natural phenomenon. This format typically involves some supernatural forces, such as gods and goddesses. Let's look at a Greek myth meant to explain the existence of the spider.

The goddess Athena was a consummate weaver of tapestries. A human woman challenged Athena to a weaving contest to prove who was the more talented. Athena wove a spectacular tapestry, but she was forced to admit that the mortal weaver's skill and talent surpassed her own. However, the subject matter chosen by the woman offended Athena. The weaver used a theme intended to mock the gods and their folly, and one of the gods she derided was Athena's own father Zeus. Athena was so enraged at this expression of disrespect that she turned the woman into a spider. Of course, today we know the spider as the ultimate weaver. That human woman's name was Arachne, and this is the origin of our word for the class of invertebrate animals known as arachnids, to which the spider belongs.

Stories that are seen as historical, but that may be questionable in their veracity are, as they say, the stuff of legend. A legend is often handed down from generation to generation through an oral tradition. It can have varying versions and can change over time. The legends of Camelot and King Arthur are a perfect example of this genre of storytelling. These tales are in no way proprietary. The original author may be unknown, but the stories endure. The tales are told and retold from family member to family member, from performer to listener, from playwright to audience. With each telling comes a nuance of change—an insight into a character's motivation or a side tale that helps to explain the plot. Often a legend will become a lexicon of a culture.

The Arthurian legend of Camelot originated in the Celtic lands, in what is now part of the United Kingdom. But the stories are so pervasive and well known among people everywhere that there was a habit in the early 1960s in the United States of referring to the presidential administration of John F. Kennedy as Camelot. This reflected the association people made between Kennedy's leadership and that of King Arthur as the epitome of benevolence, bravery, and wisdom. Very often a legend will embody the ideals of a society.

And now we come to my favorite: the fairytale. The fairytale, sometimes referred to as a wonder tale, is a story set in an indefinite place and time depicting supernatural events and archetypal characters. The Princess is meant to live happily ever after with the Prince. The ogre will try to destroy what is good. There are magical helpers and evil stepmothers. There are false heroes and true knights, fairies who might cause mischief or bring a valuable gift. The world of fairytales is fluid, wondrous, and unreal. They are a lovely and sometimes welcome escape from our mundane lives.

But make no mistake: fairytales hold Truths. In most fairytales the characters, events, and magical beings are metaphors for real lives.

All powerful stories contain characters that can be seen as archetypes. The word *archetype* first entered the English language in the 1500s. It derives from the Latin meaning "first molded" and draws some meaning from the Greek *archetupon*, which, roughly translated, means "original pattern or prototype."

Noted psychologist Carl Jung used the term *archetype* to describe a universal idea or pattern of thought to illustrate certain traits of the human psyche. The most readily understood Jungian archetype is that of "Mother." Presented with the idea of "Mother," we can all come up with the characteristics that define it. Some will say that Mother means love and nurturing and protection. We will agree that the Mother is the feminine parental figure, who gives birth, feeds, protects, and nurtures her young. Yet some will tell you that Mother means overprotective, manipulative, and meddlesome. Some believe Mother to be overbearing and controlling. This aspect is known as the Shadow.

Each archetype (e.g., Mother, Father, Warrior, Orphan, Hero, Lover, Sage—to name a few) has its Shadow side. And these different aspects of character can be incorporated into story. It is often these light and shadow aspects of an archetype that make a story meaningful.

A Warrior who dwells mostly in the Shadow aspects of violence and aggression at the beginning of the story may transform into the heroic aspect of the archetype who protects the innocent and wins the day for his people at the end.

The Sage who takes advantage of his students and egotistically revels in their worship may find some deeper meaning for his work and bestow some life-changing wisdom on those who look to him for answers.

This shows the powerful presence of archetypes in story. And each genre of story will have its own archetypes.

An example of an archetype in fable would be the Tortoise. The Tortoise is the Underdog: that figure who is unlikely to win out, but is most wanted to, due to his character and likability.

In myth, gods and goddesses are generally presented as archetypes, although many gods or goddesses represent multiple archetypes. The Norse god Odin, for example, is the Sage who sacrifices for his wisdom. The story goes that, in search of true wisdom, Odin hung himself from the world tree Yggdrasil. He sacrificed an eye to the Well of Mimir for true sight. His wisdom and commitment placed him as the "Allfather" among his people. He is also seen as a great Warrior.

In fairytales there are additional archetypes. There is a word for *witch* in every language. This archetype is usually seen as wicked and evil, especially in more recent writings. But, thanks to L. Frank Baum, we have at least one example in Glinda showing that some witches can be good.

Even though we may see these characters as fictional, there are still traits and personalities that go with each one. A Troll hides under a bridge and preys upon those who cross, especially if they're weak. Picture a corrupt businessman who takes advantage of his clients. An Ogre terrorizes the village or demands a sacrifice. Imagine a mob boss who frightens local business owners and extorts their profits. A Princess is usually innocent and victimized. This may correlate to the young and naive college student caught in some frat-house nightmare. Queens can be either noble and regal—a single mom who provides for her children and makes sacrifices for their good—or evil and vain—a selfish and shallow celebrity who will harm others for her own aggrandizement.

You can see how these archetypal characters, although they are magical and fictitious, can be correlated to real people, with real struggles.

These are just some of the archetypal images that can be pulled out of the genre of fairytale.

ARCHETYPE EXERCISE

Perhaps some of these archetypes match the personalities of the people in your real-life story. Begin to consider this. Who in your story might be the Ogre, the Evil Queen, the Witch, or the heroic Prince or Princess? Spend about fifteen minutes writing about this. Cast yourself as a character also, if you wish.

These are themes that are repeated throughout the history of fairytale. And all of these, plus many others, can be incorporated into your own tale.

In the next chapter, we will take a closer look at the genre of fairytale. We will discover that many of the stories we are familiar with have a much richer—and perhaps darker—past than in their popular versions. You may think of fairytales as just for children. You may think of them as innocent and light. But you will discover that there is no tale too dark and scary for the fairytale. Be brave, dear reader, and press on.

CHAPTER 5

୨ଢ଼ଢ଼ଌ

FAIRYTALES:
THE MAGICKAL AND THE MUNDANE

As we laid out in the previous chapter, there are many genres of story. But for the practice of Storytelling Alchemy, we will be working with fairytales. In this chapter, we will explore some familiar fairytales and some new ones. You'll discover deeper meanings and a darker history—some, in fact, that may even match your own.

The Merriam-Webster dictionary defines a *fairytale* as: 1) "a story (as for children) involving fantastic forces and beings (as fairies, wizards, and goblins), called also fairy story, or 2) a story in which improbable events lead to a happy ending."

Most fairytales contain certain basic elements. Fairytales generally begin and end with special words or phrases like "once upon a time" and "happily ever after." There is usually some kind of conflict between good and evil. There are often castles, magical realms, and otherworldly creatures. And there is a message. The fairytale tends to take us out of the mundane reality of our lives. It involves magic and supernatural forces. But while our human desire for escapism and entertainment draws us in, these stories ultimately also contain some universal truth. This is their true appeal: everyone can relate to the characters or to their situations.

Even though we are not mermaids, we can identify with a young person who desires to change her life and establish her independence from her parents.

Even though we are not ducklings or swans, we certainly recognize the feeling of being different and not fitting in.

The fairytale can explore all aspects of the human struggle. And many of the ones we know well explore a number of struggles in a single story.

Cinderella was orphaned, then enslaved and mistreated, helped by benevolent others, and then experienced triumph and true love.

Little Red Riding Hood had to take care of an invalid family member. She experienced fear of the unknown in the forest. She faced deception by an evil and shady character. She even confronted certain annihilation—in the earlier tellings, anyway.

Beyond the definition of the fairytale, beyond the pieces that make up this genre of story, are the elements of life. They contain grief and sadness, fear and real danger, love and hope, anger and hatred, comedy and tragedy. I chose the fairytale genre because, whatever *your* personal story is, it can be fictionalized using this format because fairytales cover the entire gamut of human emotion and experience. They teach us lessons and give us a reason to cheer for the "good guy." They ignite our empathy with the characters and can show us that maybe there are magical solutions to hope for. (Hint, dear reader: there are.)

There are certain elements of fairytales that I believe lend themselves well to the process of healing. Those magical solutions involve transformation—a pumpkin turns into a coach; a mouse, to a footman. Anytime we succeed in changing something at depth in our worldview, we have performed this alchemical transmutation.

Let's explore a few of the more popular fairytales to get a feeling for how they may be of use in your own alchemical journey.

Often we are familiar with the most modern telling of a story. Our society—especially western society—seems to have boiled down these sweeping and deeply meaningful tales to very simplistic, easily digestible children's stories, but many of them did not start that way.

We begin with "The Little Mermaid." The version that most of us are familiar with is the Disney movie—as is the case with many popular fairytales.

But the original "Little Mermaid," penned by Hans Christian Andersen and first published in 1837, is quite a different story. The young mermaid still lives under the sea with her father the mer-king. She still longs for a life on land, falls for a handsome prince, trades with the sea witch, and sacrifices her beautiful voice for human legs. But that is about where the similarities end.

In Andersen's version, the little mermaid has a much deeper longing than just for that handsome prince. She has been told by her grandmother that humans live shorter life spans than mermaids, who can live for about three hundred years. But the little mermaid learns that when a human dies, her eternal soul goes on forever. When a mermaid dies, she simply turns into sea foam and ceases to be. The little mermaid longs to become human in order to obtain that immortal soul. This deep motivation brings her to the desperate trade with the sea witch.

The price she paid for her legs was also much greater than just her lovely voice. The process would be excruciatingly painful, as if a sword were passing through her body. And even though her legs would help her to dance more beautifully than any human ever had, with every step she would always feel as though she were walking on daggers. She accepted this price, not for a prince, but for the hope of possessing a soul. She is told that she will have her soul if she can make the prince fall in love with her and marry her. But if the prince marries another, the little mermaid's life would end, without a soul, at dawn after the prince's wedding.

In the Disney version, we are treated to that happily ever after— not so in the original. Through a case of mistaken identity, the prince falls for and marries someone else, and the little mermaid is left to contemplate her fate in the coming dawn.

In the night, the little mermaid's sisters, fearing her end, also make a bargain with the sea witch. They trade their beautiful hair for an enchanted dagger and they bring it to the little mermaid. She is told that if she uses this dagger to kill the prince before dawn, she may return to the sea and live out her natural mermaid life. But her heart is filled with mercy and she cannot kill the sleeping prince, even in the face of her own death.

In the end, as the little mermaid senses herself transforming into sea foam, she realizes that she can still feel the sunshine and that she has not ceased to be. Soon she is joined by others who are called the daughters of air. They tell her that because of her mercy and her sacrifices, she may still reach her goal of obtaining an immortal soul if she performs good deeds for humans for the next three hundred years.

All of this rich imagery and deep emotion—and all of the tragedy—was sanitized for the Disney film audience. This story is so much more than the shallow "princess-finds-her-prince" tale that we know.

You'll note that there's quite a bit of darkness and pain in the original tale. No transformation comes without a price. So if you feared that your story is too tragic, too gory, or too horrific to put into a fairytale, read on, my friend. There are some gruesome parts to many of these stories.

In the Grimm version of Cinderella, the stepsisters went so far as to cut off their own toes in attempts to make their feet fit into the prince's glass slipper. The prince was alerted to their ruse by the blood pouring out of it!

In a still earlier version of the tale from China, Cinderella was called Ye Xian. Ye Xian's only friend was a beautiful fish with golden eyes. She would share her food with the fish, although she had little for herself. Her stepmother knew of her love for the fish, and she killed it and cooked it for a meal. (I find it interesting to note the Chinese origins of this tale. Recall the ancient practice of binding girls' feet and the concept equating tiny feet with beauty.)

In the Grimm version of "Little Red Riding Hood," the wolf actually did eat the grandmother and Little Red. And then a hunter came along and gutted the wolf, allowing the two to tumble out. Gross, right?

Whatever darkness there may be in your personal story, it can be incorporated into a real fairytale in some way—and I will help you do that.

I want to share with you an example of a fairytale with an empowering outcome to give you an idea of how to transmute the tragedy of the SYTY into your own new empowering fairytale.

There's a beautiful Japanese fairytale now known as "The Boy Who Drew Cats." It was translated by Lafcadio Hearn and published in 1898 as number 23 of Hasegawa Takejirō's *Japanese Fairy Tale Series*. I retell it here in my own words. This is an empowering tale about staying true to yourself and your talents. I say it's about following your bliss, à la Joseph Campbell.

There was a little boy in Japan, who was one of many children in a farming family. All the children were expected to help and contribute to the family business. But this little boy was frail and weak, and the only thing he liked to do was draw cats. His family found him to be a financial burden. While he was frail and weak, he was quite clever, so the family decided to send him away to a temple to have him train as an apprentice to a monk.

While he was at the temple, he studied, but he also continued to draw his cats. He drew them everywhere, in sketch pads, on walls, anywhere he could. And even though the monk would scold him and tell him to stop, he just could not stop drawing cats. Eventually, the monk decided that he was not apprentice material and prepared to send the boy back to his family.

But the boy didn't want to go home to his family and be seen as a failure. He didn't want them to be ashamed of him. So he left the temple in search of a way that he could be successful somehow. He hoped that he could perhaps find another temple and do better next time. When he left, the monk warned him to avoid wide-open spaces and told him to "Keep to the small."

The boy set off on his journey and eventually came upon a village late at night where he found a temple in the center of town. Everything was very quiet. The boy entered the temple and called out, but no one answered. He decided to stay the night and seek out the village folk in the morning.

He stepped into the great room of the temple and was astonished to find a vast room with beautiful, large rice-paper screens adorning every wall—blank screens, empty screens. The little boy couldn't resist, and he whiled away the hours drawing the largest cats he'd ever drawn all over the screens of the temple until he was surrounded by enormous cats.

STORYTELLING ALCHEMY

By this time, the boy was getting sleepy. He was about to doze off when he remembered the monk's warning about wide-open spaces. This temple room was very large, so he looked around and found a small cabinet. He crawled inside, closed the door, and fell fast asleep.

What the sleeping boy did not know was that this village was abandoned because of a great goblin rat who lived in the temple. The goblin rat had terrorized the town until all the villagers had fled.

In the night, the boy suddenly awoke to loud and horrible sounds coming from the temple room. There was a great racket and noises of a fierce battle. There was growling and screaming. The sounds were so terrible that the boy didn't even dare to look. He simply hid in his cabinet, held his breath, and waited and prayed for the violence to stop.

In the morning, it was quiet again, and the boy summoned the courage to come out of his hiding place. As he emerged from the cabinet, he saw a giant dead goblin rat in the middle of the large temple room, lying in a pool of its own blood. But there was nothing else there.

The little boy wondered what could've happened. He wondered what caused the great battle sounds of the previous night and what killed this great big scary goblin rat.

But then he noticed that all of his cat drawings had blood on their mouths and claws. And the truth of it dawned on him. The cats that he had drawn had come to life in the middle of the night and slayed that horrible goblin rat.

Once the villagers learned of this, the boy became a national hero. He was praised for his talent and his abilities. He brought the honor that he had hoped for to his family. That little boy grew up to be a famous and successful artist who only *drew cats. And it is said that his art is still displayed, revered, and admired to this day.*

I love this story because, even in the face of family shame, even in the face of all manner of possible trouble, the boy never gave up his true passion. He never changed what he was. And that is precisely what saved him in the end. It is an allegory for the currently popular concept of living your most authentic life. It is a metaphor for "following your bliss," as taught by Joseph Campbell, who said:

If you do follow your bliss, you put yourself on a kind of track that has been there all the while, waiting for you, and the life that you ought to be living is the one you are living. Follow your bliss and don't be afraid, and doors will open where you didn't know they were going to be.[1]

These are the kinds of stories that can teach us and change us.

FAIRYTALE EXERCISE

Take your journal to your sacred space; become mindful and present. Make your offerings and think about the fairytales that you remember from childhood. Did you identify with the characters? Which ones fascinated or terrified you? Which ones made you *feel* something? Which stories just gave you a sense of wonder? Which stories did you love? Spend twenty to thirty minutes writing about the fairytales you remember. Allow your writing to be free and to explore whatever ideas and feelings are evoked.

---

1. This is a quote from *The Power of Myth*, a series of interviews with Joseph Campbell by Bill Moyers. It originally aired on PBS in 1988.

Look a little further into the origins of the stories you recall during the exercise. You may find a deeper and richer journey with which to identify. You may find that the tale, as told and orally passed down from generation to generation before it was ever written, may have a deep message for you.

GOOGLE ASSIGNMENT

Consult the "Great Oracle of Google" and see what more you can find about your favorite childhood fairytales. What you discover may give you some insight into the work to come. Do a little research and find something rich in those old tales.

Now that we've learned a bit about the dark side of the fairytale genre, let's examine the reasons that this particular variety of storytelling can help you emerge from your chrysalis as the butterfly you deserve to be. In the next chapter, we will explore all the reasons this will work for you. Turn the page.

CHAPTER 6

꧁

FAIRYTALE FORMAT
AND ALCHEMY

Let's explore the reasons why fairytales are the best choice for your transformation. In this chapter we'll discover the many ways that telling your story in this format is healing and enlightening.

And, on the subject of enlightenment, let's talk alchemy, that medieval "science" of turning lead into gold. Today the word has come to be understood as a profound transformation.

ALCHEMY

The practice and philosophies of alchemy reach back thousands of years and span the globe. Evidence has been found of some form of philosophy whereby base metals can be transmuted into nobler metals in ancient China, Hellenistic Egypt, and ancient India.

The principles and experimentation that accompanied the early practitioners' work in the transmutation of physical metals are seen today as a sort of prototype for modern chemistry. The words *alchemy* and *chemistry* derive from the same roots, most probably from *chymeia*, the ancient Greek word for "mixture."

It was the understanding of early alchemists that all of matter is, in fact, made up of one thing—the Prima Materia—manifested in different ways to produce the perceptions that cause us to see gold as different from lead. In the alchemist's view, these things were intrinsically alike and therefore, given the right set of circumstances, could be transmuted one into the other.

Alchemists also believed strongly that this world (i.e., earth, life as we know it, etc.) is a reflection and manifestation of the divine world. We were made in God's image, and our existence was made in the image of God's existence, or paradise. As above, so below. Therefore, it was our purpose—even our responsibility—to elevate all that there is here to the level of perfection occupied by that Source.

Carl Jung has explored correlations between alchemy and his psychoanalytic process, known as individuation. His belief was that the practice of alchemy was a process for uncovering the unconscious Shadow and making it conscious or bringing it into the light. The "Great Work" of alchemy was a process by which the individual could turn the lead of this unconscious into the gold of the whole Self.

Jung's philosophy was that each person contains an unconscious that desires to be integrated with the conscious and thus make the Self one. He believed that this form of consciousness was the way to create the whole world anew and complete the work begun by God when he breathed life into the first humans.

Remember when I discussed deeply held beliefs? (Please see page 13 for a refresher.) This is what Jung means when he refers to the Shadow and to integrating that with the conscious mind and forming the "Whole Self." Bringing those ideas into the light of consciousness and accepting them are the work of this book and the Great Work of the alchemists.

It is thought that many of the ancient alchemists believed in the possibility of the literal, physical transmutation of lead into gold *and* that this transmutation would prove the ability of humans to rise to the level of God in his enlightenment. Some scholars on this subject have put forth the idea that the desire to complete the physical transmutation of the metals was not sufficient to accomplish it, even if the alchemist had the chemistry in perfect order. This theory states that the alchemist had to have devoted his life to God and must want the gold only as a symbol of man's ability to perfect his own nature in a similar way.

Jung's understanding of the Great Work was characterized by a kind of mirroring effect. The alchemists of old, in performing these experiments on chemical compounds, were actually projecting their own unconscious onto the work at hand, and therefore, the outcomes that they perceived were simply mirrors of the unconscious in its desire to be made conscious. Jung believed that alchemy was a symbolic work intended to achieve the integration of the Shadow into the conscious mind. He believed that the observer's view could not be separated from the object being viewed and therefore influenced what the alchemist saw. (And of course, this has been confirmed by modern physics.)

In this sense, Jung believed that everything that the human consciousness perceives is a mirror of the unconscious, or Shadow, trying to be discovered. In fact, the etymology of the word for *mirror*, in some languages, translates to "shadow."

Lately, scientific discoveries seem to support the idea that all matter is made up of the same energy. This would seem to indicate that even our state of mind, our relationship to the universe, and our deeply held beliefs can be transmuted from negative and limiting to positive and empowering.

There are still those today who practice alchemy in its esoteric, or hidden, form. These practitioners seek their own enlightenment and transformation of the spirit. They seek throughout their lives to reach their highest human potential. They take on the Great Work as the pivotal tool to bring about their own enlightenment. And the culmination of this process is known as the philosopher's stone.

The mythical philosopher's stone was said to be a substance that could be used to heal all ills and even bestow immortality. One small sliver of the philosopher's stone was said to have properties that could transmute large quantities of a base metal, such as lead or tin, into precious metals like silver or gold.

In the modern alchemist's pursuit of enlightenment, the philosopher's stone can be likened to that place in one's soul that propels one to greatness. That powerful and magical talisman can be found nowhere but within. And the search that leads us to it is nothing short of a lifetime's work. This, to me, is the discovery of the True Will.

You may uncover a number of different "philosopher's stones" throughout your journey to become a more enlightened human being. At times, it will be education that moves you toward a truer understanding of the world around you. Sometimes it is the simple joy of doing what you love to the best of your ability. That feeling of being "in the zone" when you are accomplishing something can be truly life-enhancing. And that sensation is the best indication that you are acting in alignment with your True Will.

There are even times throughout life when suffering and hardship themselves represent the philosopher's stone. We learn and grow from those experiences, of course, but it may take some framing of our perception of the suffering in order for us to understand it better and move away from the pain and into the intended lesson. And that is where Storytelling Alchemy comes in.

THE POWER OF FAIRYTALES

So why have I chosen the fairytale as the philosopher's stone of Storytelling Alchemy? What can be gained from taking our truly harrowing experiences and reducing them to a child's fantasy?

First and foremost, this genre lends itself to healing old hurts precisely because it *is* fantasy. Take a few moments to remember what it was like when you were a child and listening to a fairytale. There was no need for any conscious "suspension of disbelief." You were sucked in and totally on board. There was wonder, and there was openness. In this way, the conscious mind is entertained while the unconscious mind is enlightened.

What we are trying to do is reach and influence those limiting beliefs that have become so engrained that they are now operating unconsciously within us.

Here's a little exercise. Raise your right hand. Yes, now. Do it. Did you? Okay, good.

Now, did you do that consciously or unconsciously?

When I ask this question in live workshops, most people will say they did it consciously. They had a conscious thought to raise their arm and then it happened, right?

Wrong. We wouldn't get much done at all if we had to actually, consciously think out all the necessary processes that take place when we raise our arms. In truth, it takes a billion electrical connections, firing synapses, muscles, and tendons working in a precise sequence to equal "raised arm." We did not consciously think through all of that. We simply thought, "raise arm," and it happened.

A whole different billion electrical impulses and movements in sequence equal walking, opening a door, typing, etc., etc. Imagine if we had to do all that with conscious thinking.

Now . . . think about the power of the unconscious mind, the part of your mind that *is* doing that much processing and producing the desired result in an *instant*. How long would it take us to consciously think through all of that? And how quickly does it happen for us. *That's* the power difference between our conscious and unconscious minds.

So what role do you think the unconscious mind might play in your daily life? If you hold an unconscious assumption (i.e., a deeply held belief) that was implanted in you in early childhood that, for example, you are not very bright, you are making decisions for yourself based upon that assumption. It may have been placed in your psyche by an angry teacher or a mean cousin or even a well-meaning parent. And you will not be consciously aware that you hold this belief. But make no mistake: it is limiting your potential.

A person who holds such a belief will pass up an opportunity to take college courses or unconsciously overlook a classified ad for a job that requires more thinking than physical work. Such a person will defer to others in situations they could have potentially solved themselves. And they won't even know why.

These kinds of limiting beliefs were forged in your most painful moments, in those stories that you repeat about your past. Those SYTY dwell on the pain of "what happened to you" and "who did this to you." That's where those deeply held, *and almost certainly false,* beliefs were born. Then, throughout your life, these false beliefs are nurtured, developed, and planted deep within the feeling part of you by your own retelling of the story—whether to yourself or others—over and over again.

Bringing those beliefs to the surface and proving them wrong are the whole focus of the Storytelling Alchemy practice.

In order to reach that unconscious part of our psyche, we must bring back our childlike wonder. We need that emotional acceptance of the events being told. We need our egoic, thinking, rational mind to get out of the way so that our soulful, nonjudgmental, feeling, healing heart can go to work on our perceived limitations.

The fairytale is a great vehicle for this also because there is no construct of logic that must be followed. Your characters can be animals who can speak or trolls under bridges or fairies or elves or witches and wizards. Your setting can be deep in an enchanted forest or under the sea or in a vast desert or on another planet or inside a speck of dust under the foot of your dining room table. With fairytales there is no limitation to how you can reframe your own past.

Magic is available to you in this format. You don't have to worry about how you could possibly make a positive outcome from such a negative event. The wave of a wand or the touch of a talisman—or a fairy godmother—can change anything and everything.

And when you begin to formulate your new story, the process of opening your mind to this magical potential is part of the way the message can reach that soulful heart.

By employing a willingness to immerse yourself and your story into this world of wonder and whimsy, you also begin to gain a bit of emotional distance to make room for the healing that must come.

Healing can be painful. And what we "know" about our past can sometimes feel too painful to contemplate deeply. As I've said before, simply reliving that old hurt is not productive but rather destructive. But reviewing and examining it in the more objective way needed to change it and create Your Fairytale can move you forward toward that healing.

Sometimes, when a patient has a very serious injury or illness, doctors will actually place the patient in a medically induced coma so that they aren't spending their healing energy dealing with so much pain. Along the same lines, changing your story into a fairytale puts that little bit of space between you and the pain of your history. And in that space your mind can formulate new ideas and opinions about it, bringing lasting change.

And here's another thought about lightening the burden of that healing process: What's wrong with a little harmless revenge exacted on an old enemy by making them the ogre in the story? Cast your ex as the hideous swamp goblin that terrorizes the village. Give your abuser the role of wicked witch, with *extra* warts! Adding a little levity and humor is always an aid in the healing process. After all, laughter is the best medicine!

In fairytales, as we've discussed, there exist outrageous story lines and crazy things happen that include sorrow, loss, tragedy, resilience, redemption, and triumph. None of it is shocking because we know it's a wonder tale. We don't reject the idea that someone could be turned into a toad by the evil witch, for instance.

And while we're on the subject of being turned into a toad, let's explore a couple of examples of changing a real-life story into a fairytale. You need to explore the underlying emotions, the basic characteristics of the fairytale character's predicament, and see if you can find the correlations in real life that fit the story.

What happens to a person who has been turned into a toad? They lose their ability to communicate. They lose their voice. They cannot move around the world as they once did. They've been rendered small and insignificant. They've been made into something that is ugly and shunned.

Now think about a woman who has married an abusive man. He doesn't value her opinions and doesn't listen to her when she speaks to him. (Lost voice.) He dictates to her exactly where she may go and when she is permitted to leave the house. (Lost mobility.) He demeans and degrades her in front of others. (Made small.) He raises horrid bruises on her skin when he beats her. (Made ugly.)

Are you beginning to see how these stories can correlate to your own?

Let's try another example. A young man climbs a beanstalk, or passes through a portal of some kind, and finds himself in a world of giants, who might step on him or, worse, cook him in a stew and eat him for supper! He is in an alien world, feeling lost and fearful. He doesn't know what dangers await. He is, by turns, ignored, harmed by neglect, and actively attacked. He doesn't seem to have the power to return to his world and safety.

A boy in foster care is brought to a new home. (Alien world.) His foster family is only taking in children for the governmental check that each one generates. Not only are they not interested in his welfare, they are abusive. (Generating fear.) So are some of the other fostered children. (Many possible dangers.) His foster father is a pedophile. (To be cooked and eaten.)

In these examples, you can see how you may begin to find fairytale scenarios that fit your story. Your own fairytale will be *your* truth couched and cushioned in fiction. It is also a way for you to find those falsehoods that were engrained in your unconscious and bring them to the light so that they can be destroyed. With a fairytale, you can cut open that bad wolf to restore what was taken from you.

FAIRYTALE ASSOCIATION EXERCISE

In this instance, it is important that you ground yourself by acknowledging and becoming mindful of the beauty of your sacred space. Make your offerings and ask to be allowed to feel safe and emotionally removed from the images that might arise during this exercise.

Spend some time trying to correlate the stories and characters of your own life to the archetypes and typical narrative of fairytales that you know. Try to match a few different SYTY with these familiar tales. Feel free to break this exercise down into several sessions.

Now that you have a storytelling foundation, let's get back to the mechanics of the writing and exercises that you've been diligently performing. In the next chapter, we will explore the need for review of your storytelling journal and the things that you've discovered. Writing it all down is helpful, but it's in the review and understanding that you will find your inspiration, self-knowledge, and healing.

CHAPTER 7

REVIEW AND REVEAL

You have been faithfully keeping a record of this journey in your storytelling journal and that is a valuable task, but it becomes so much more meaningful if you go back and reread what you've written.

Let's review and learn about you!

A LOOK BACK AT JOURNALING

Throughout this process, you've been recording your impressions, memories, dreams, etc., in your journal. If you've done that, no doubt there is quite a bit of material built up at this point.

The writing itself is therapeutic. But the rereading of the things you've written can show your progress, and that is encouraging. It can illuminate the changes you've already experienced with this process or remind you of ideas that you'd forgotten.

Take some time to reread your journal and everything that you've recorded so far. This may spark new insights. Write those down too!

Write in the margins of past entries, or star the location and take up a new page for new ideas and understandings.

As you review what you've written so far, try to take the perspective of a loving, benevolent friend who may not be familiar with all of the context of the events that sparked your words.

Elaborate wherever necessary to make the entries clear and understandable. Again, write in margins or expand your impressions and ideas on a new page in your book if you need more space.

Some of your entries and exercises may have sparked some research—into fairytales, into storytelling, your heritage, or your own personal history. If there are things you've discovered about your journey not contained in the journal, add them now.

If you've noticed a shift in your understanding of certain SYTY or a new perspective into the characters who've played a role, record that. Comment on your progress. Write down your impressions of the ways in which you've changed since embarking on this weird journey.

Review the things you've written about your dreams. Contemplate whether the imagery there can be included or influence Your Fairytale. You may have noticed that your dreams are not terribly literal. Dreams speak to us in symbols, in the same way that fairytales do.

DREAM INTERPRETATION, PART TWO

Let's take a moment to tread a little deeper into dream interpretation, now that you've hopefully got some of yours written down.

Your dreams take on the language that you feed them. You may have noticed that after binge-watching a show like *Supernatural* or *Game of Thrones*, that characters, circumstances, and symbols from those shows appear in your dreams.

Example: In my twenties, I recall attending a party where we played charades for hours. A crowd of young people drank and play-acted from about lunchtime through to the wee hours of the morning. For several nights afterward, my dreams were all in the form of charades. My unconscious psyche was letting me know that the psychological issue it was working on had something to do with a book title, consisting of four words, which a person might mime by drawing an arc in the air and spinning in circles as though caught in some wind. I did eventually figure out that this was meant to depict *The Wizard of Oz*, but what that actually meant for me, I did not know.

The meanings of our dreams can be a bit vague and difficult to pinpoint. Just know that they speak a symbolic language. And anything that you've encountered, studied, or obsessed about is fair game for your unconscious to dredge up as a representation of its message for you.

For instance, I study Tarot. This system of divination has been a big part of my life for a very long time. Very frequently my dreams will include images of Tarot cards. Sometimes the personifications of the cards play a role in my dreams. I love it when this happens because each single image or idea, such as the Magician or the Priestess, contains so many layers of meaning, and because I "speak the language," it becomes easy for me to interpret what is being shown to me.

If there is some system of knowledge with which you are familiar, you can use that to help your subconscious send you clearer messages. For example, if you are a gardener, you may see certain plants in your dreams. When you do, remember to take in all of the possible meanings that this plant might have for you. Is it edible? What kinds of things can you cook with it? Is it a flowering plant? What colors? What is your relationship to this plant in your own garden? Does it flourish or is it a little more difficult to keep growing?

With a single image, your psyche has revealed to you all of these things that may be important to your journey. You can also give your subconscious the suggestion before you go to sleep to include some symbols from your particular expertise and then see what happens!

Although Jung delved deeply into dream interpretation, he believed that our dreams do their work regardless of whether or not we understand them. But within the practice of Storytelling Alchemy, I find that dreams can be extremely helpful.

As you review the dreams you've recorded in your journal, take special note of those that involve similar situations, characters, or feelings as any of the SYTY that you may want to work with. Review those dreams with a little more attention and in a bit more depth than the others. These may give you inspiration for Your Fairytale or insight into some aspect of the events that actually took place.

If there appear to be unfinished details or questions that were posed but not answered in these dreams, focus on those and perform the following exercise with these things in mind.

In reviewing your notes and returning to the things that you've learned, experienced, and questioned, you may find that there are parts of the SYTY that you simply can't understand. Your introspections and your dreams may have failed to give you the answers you desire.

For example, there may have been a person involved in your story whose motives just don't make sense to you. There may be a period of time that your conscious mind simply will not remember.

Once again, use the power of suggestion on your mind before you go to sleep. Prompt yourself as you fall asleep to learn the perspective and motivations of that other person, or set for yourself the intention that you will remember in your dreams what you could not recall during your waking hours.

DREAM INTERPRETATION EXERCISE

Go to your sacred space with your journal open to the page with the dream entry to be explored. Perform your usual ritual of offerings and breathing, and become mindful and still.

In your mind's eye, place yourself back in the dream in the place and time where the question arises. If a character has done something that confuses you, visualize them before you now, and ask them to explain.

If, in the dream, you performed an action that seemed unfinished or there was a mystery you could not see, imagine now that you can see it and understand its message for you.

Play your dreams out to their conclusions in a waking but meditative and imaginative state, and you may find answers you did not know existed.

Allow yourself to come back to your body and your beautiful sacred space feeling refreshed and relaxed.

Write down the new insights that you've gained from "finishing" your dreams in this way.

When you wake up, write down your impressions.

Remember to continue to review your journal from time to time. This practice will allow you new insights and perhaps just give you a reason to recognize and honor your progress, resilience, and courage. And it is very important to do that in this practice and in life. Remember and acknowledge that you are *awesome*!

Now, where is all this magick I've been promising you? In the next chapter we will explore the ways you may boost your progress and enhance your outcomes with spellcraft and thinking magickally. We'll explore some basic tenets of magickal workings, and I'll give you examples of workings I have performed in order to achieve my desires.

CHAPTER 8

SERIOUS SPELLS, SIGILS, AND HYPERSIGILS

First, let's get very basic. What is a spell? At the risk of oversimplification, I'll start with what I have always told my newbie students, strangers who've asked, and those not necessarily steeped in the world of witchcraft. I would tell them that a spell is like a prayer you can touch. In its simplest form, a spell is an expression of a personal desire with an intention to bring it about, in the form of clearly stating intentions, taking certain actions, and utilizing some earthly materials.

The earliest form of this type of spell is easily recognizable to just about every child. It's your birthday! Here's your cake with candles matching the number of years you're celebrating (perhaps including one extra "for luck"). Make a wish and blow out the candles! That's a spell.

A spell is a way of connecting that which is of earth with that which is divine. We humans are stardust. This has been said by hippies and scientists alike—and it's true. If we look inside, through meditation, through spiritual practice and experience, we can see our connection to divinity. But we *are* existing in this earth plane; we are material beings in this world, regardless of our spiritual truth. And we are here on this material plane for a reason. So why not acknowledge and utilize that earthly energy we've been given.

I had a teacher who shared his experiences with the realm of faerie and the realms of beings that are not material and "of earth." He always said that they were actually jealous of humans' ability to create. If an etheric entity wanted to sit down, it would manifest a seat out of the ether and sit. When it arose again, the seat would vanish, having no further need to exist. The ethereal entities expressed envy at our ability to manifest real, solid matter from our thoughts. Consider that a chair, any chair, would have never existed if not thought of first.

We are extremely powerful beings in our ability to manifest, in material reality, that which enters and takes root in our minds. Ethereal entities can seemingly manifest at will, but their manifestations are always temporary and fleeting. As humans, we have the ability to conceive of, design, and build an edifice that may stand for thousands of years. This is a great power. We should own and embrace it.

Thinking of and then building a chair seems, to us, not magickal at all. We seem to be able to trace the causal connection between the idea that sitting would be comfortable to the mind's creation of a device that could help accomplish that to the acquisition and assemblage of the actual physical bits of matter that create a piece of furniture known, today, as chair.

But our ability to connect a thought to a physical object and then make it a reality is actually very magickal indeed.

If you'd like to ponder the idea of alchemy—of turning lead to gold—think for a moment of the process it must have taken to turn a sheaf of wheat into a loaf of bread. Cooking is alchemy. And I can think of no better representation of transformation than that of the plant growing in a field, moved by the wind, and presenting itself to a human, who somehow thought, "I can transform this hard-shelled seed into a life-sustaining, deeply satisfying food that will become the staple of civilizations."

This is miraculous, really, and akin to the idea of transforming lead into gold. There may be a lot of difficult steps to the process, but aren't they worth it, considering the final result?

So, spellcraft is alchemy. We take what *is* and transform it to what is *desired*. This is the way of the witches. It has been done for thousands of years. Spells were originally cast, as discussed earlier, for the good of the hunt. Spells were cast to create new kinds of food. Spells were cast that provided humankind with choices. "Would you decide to be a nomadic hunter-gatherer or a stationary farmer of the fields?" The human Will began to create the world with these kinds of questions. We became as gods when we were able to decide our own fates.

And from this understanding of the influence of our Will on the world, we learn that we are magickal. Those individuals who have not yet come to the understanding that they are magickal and have the power to manifest their desired outcomes are still creating—but they are creating unconsciously. They are allowing their habitual thoughts, words, and actions to craft a world that may make them very unhappy. Witches and practitioners of magick, as I'm teaching here, use our power consciously. We live and manifest "on purpose." And spellcraft is one way in which we do that.

Some of our spells are quite simple, and some are more complex and far-reaching. We will delve into that later. But for now, let's stick to the basics of spellcraft.

MAKING A MOJO BAG

One of the first types of spells that most new witches learn to do is making a mojo bag. A mojo bag consists physically of a number of different items in a pouch. The basic instructions to create and empower the bag would be something like this:

Choose your intention. Make it as clear as possible.

Choose your materials based on your intent.

Perform a ritual to "charge" the bag and its contents.

Wear the bag or keep it close or in a particular place related to your intention until your desire comes about.

I'll use an example to elaborate each of these directions and to give you an idea of how basic spellcraft works.

I made a mojo bag last year with the intention of filling up a women's retreat I was hosting. Sign-ups started out well, but as I approached the "No refund of deposit" deadline, I noticed there were still two to four spots that needed to be filled in order to reach the goals that I had set for myself. These are the steps I took to create my mojo bag:

Choose your intention. Make it as clear as possible.

I started with: "Two, three, or four ladies will discover the desire and means to attend my retreat and will sign up and pay for their spots before the deposit deadline." Then I thought about that for a little while. The first thing I noticed was that I had phrased my intent in the future tense! Whoops! Big mistake! An intent has to be a definite, present-tense statement: This *is*, not this *will be*, because if something "will be," it's never *now*. Second, I realized that I wanted four ladies—not two, not three, but four—signed up. I also decided that I wanted my retreat to be filled with a certain kind of woman. So, I refined my intention: "Four earthbound goddesses, ready to realize their power, are signed up and paid in full, for their participation in my Goddess Retreat." That is exactly how specific you need to be with your intentions when casting spells. It's a scary thing to get that specific, but I've found that it works best this way.

Choose your materials based on your intent.

I had my specific intent. What materials would go into my bag? For that matter, what kind of bag should I choose?

As I've mentioned previously, everything is made up of energy. The differentiation between the things that we perceive is often said to show that different "things" are energies vibrating at different frequencies. So, we use material objects in spells to harness their energies for our magick.

This concept of using materials in spellwork goes back to that Law of Similarity. Everything is connected. Our intention is connected to our outcome in just the same way that an acorn is connected to the mighty oak tree that it will one day be. And when we choose the materials that will represent our intention, we want them to correspond to the outcome.

My chosen outcome involved prosperity and abundance in that I was reaching for financial and career goals. My chosen outcome also included sisterhood, spiritual understanding, and love. The goal of my retreat was to help the participants uncover and work with their inner goddess. I had to pick materials that would correspond in some way with all of those wishes.

First, I chose a small, green velvet mojo bag that had an image of a goddess on it. Green has correspondences to money and prosperity. Green also has correspondence to the heart and loving kindness.

And what would go into this bag? How many items? What kind of items?

This part varies widely. The items chosen are largely intuitive. You can include things like stones, herbs, essential oils, statements written on paper, feathers, flower petals, bones, trinkets, and any other small items you can think of that will fit in the bag. Use your imagination and do a little research to learn about crystal or herbal correspondences to help you make your choices.

When in doubt, it is always wise to come back to your intention and consider what it would look like, if it were a solid, tangible bit of matter.

I wanted four goddesses. I did a Google Image search and found a picture of four beautiful ladies in the act of embracing their own divinity—or that's what it looked like to me. I printed the image and wrote my intention on the back of the paper. That was my first item for my bag.

I wanted them to pay up front. I included a small piece of pyrite or fool's gold for its symbolic connection to prosperity. I also included some gold-tone coins that I believe were arcade tokens. I keep these for just this sort of purpose. The "fool's gold" stone symbolized prosperity, but the coins represent actual *commerce* and *payment*.

Next, I wanted to include something that would stand in for my desires around the purpose of the retreat. I started with white rose petals. These represent the pure love that would flow between all of the participants. Then I was seeking something to symbolize their desire and readiness to grow and change. Hmmm . . .

Sometimes, when I have trouble finding something meaningful I resort to child's play! I like to use polymer clay to make little figurines small enough for a mojo bag. I crafted a small green chrysalis from the clay and a tiny butterfly to represent the transformation that I wanted for my clients. At that point, I felt as though I'd covered the intent and closed up the bag.

Perform a ritual to "charge" the bag and its contents.

I'm using the word *charge* here in all its meanings: First, I mean to power up the bag and its ingredients like a battery and to put the power of my Will and intention into these material objects so that they will become like a magnet for the outcome I envision. The second meaning of the word *charge* is "to instruct," similar to the way a judge charges a jury, instructing them on how to deliberate the case at hand. And finally, I am "charging" my mojo bag with an obligation to perform the magick.

The ritual can be similar to what you do when you make offerings. For this particular spell, I decided to work with the planetary deity Venus and had been making offerings to her for a few weeks leading up to the ritual. I arranged for some special offerings. Venus is a deity that values love and beauty, so sweet things, flowers, beautiful gems, and music are all appropriate.

I offered chocolate-covered strawberries and beautiful fresh roses and decided to dance with my mojo bag to the song "Venus" by Bananarama. The ritual went something like this:

I chose a Friday, because that is Venus's day.

Let me put in a word here about magickal timing. Know that the days of the week correspond to planetary deities. Monday is the

Moon, Tuesday is Mars, Wednesday is Mercury, Thursday is Jupiter, Friday is Venus, Saturday is Saturn, and Sunday is the Sun. And there are about a billion other considerations that could go into magickal timing. Some practitioners use astrology and the position of the stars and planets to determine a beneficial time for the intention of a spell. Phases of the Moon are often considered, including a time called moon void-of-course, when the moon sort of "floats" between signs of the zodiac. Some believe that magick performed or initiated during void-of-course will either fail or turn out differently than expected.

It can take years to gain an understanding of all of these aspects of timing for spellcraft. And the process can be made so complicated as to cripple the practitioner into inaction caused by fear of getting the timing wrong. Please don't allow yourself to be so caught up in this. Dive in. Perform spells, make mistakes, and learn from them. The most important thing is that you use your own intuition and understandings and approach magickal acts with a sincere desire to find genuine correspondences and improve your life.

Next, I prepared an altar on a tray including my mojo bag, the flowers and strawberries, a candle to represent Venus, and some incense. I brought everything to my outdoor ritual space along with my speaker for the music. I lit the incense and the candle and acknowledged the presence of the goddess and thanked her for the successful outcome of my spell.

One of the most important factors in spellwork is confidence in the outcome. As I said, the oak tree is in the acorn, so the answer is in the asking. I was raised Catholic and, to this day, I love the concept of prayer with confidence. I was taught as a little girl that when I prayed for something, I should immediately be thankful, even if the thing I prayed for wasn't real yet. I was told to have trust that God would handle it. I feel the same way about my magick. Once I perform the spell, I let it go. Too many practitioners will cast a spell and then wring their hands over the outcome and wonder how and when it will come. Even worse, they will wonder *if* it will come. My witchcraft works best when I "set it and forget it." If you turn on your oven to preheat it for baking a cake, you set it to the appropriate temperature and then go about the other tasks at hand, fully expecting that, when you are ready to put your prepared batter in, the oven will have reached the desired temperature. You don't stand over the oven looking at the thermometer and wondering if, when, or how it will reach 350 degrees. You just trust that it will, and it does, barring some mechanical malfunction. Magick works the same way: set it and forget it. And then be pleasantly surprised when your outcome manifests.

Anyway, back to my Venus ritual. I had my altar set up, I was in my sacred space, and I became still and quiet for a few moments as I sincerely offered the items in gratitude. I listened and meditated until I felt the time was right. Then I picked up the mojo bag and focused all of my attention and my whole Will on visualizing the perfect outcome: the four goddess/women and a successful retreat. When I felt satisfied with this, I turned on the music and danced while carrying the bag and holding my intention in my mind. When this was done, I offered thanks once more, extinguished the candle, and cleaned up the space.

Wear the bag or keep it close or in a particular place related to your intention until your desire comes about.

I chose to keep my mojo bag with me, usually tucked into my bra, close to my heart.

Within a week of that ritual and well before my deadline, I received calls and filled all four spaces with wonderful women who were an asset to the whole group during the retreat. They were so special that we've remained in touch since that time, and I cherish the goddess energy that they've cultivated for themselves.

This was a very successful spell. What I've given you above are some basic steps, but the only way to really become proficient at witchcraft and spellwork is, as with everything else that you want to master—the same way to get to Carnegie Hall: practice, practice, practice!

SIGILS

Before I have you making your own mojo bag—which will be the next exercise—I want to give you a little more background and a few extra techniques that might help you.

I told you that I wrote my intention on the back of the paper on which the goddess image was printed. Well, I left a little bit out. I wrote my intentions in a very particular way: I created a sigil.

So what exactly is a sigil? Simply put, it is a sign or a symbol. A coat of arms is a sigil that represents the entire ancestry of a family line. When you think about it, that's a powerful symbol. The images chosen for a coat of arms would include things that represent the lineage, nobility, honor, and triumphs of a whole family history.

In modern times, corporate logos are sigils. Let's take Amazon's logo, for example. First, it uses the word *Amazon*, understood to represent strength and great, imposing size. Then there is a curved line that seems to form a smile, symbolizing the happy customer, I guess. Finally, notice that the "smile line" starts at the *A* in *Amazon* and points at the *Z*. They sell everything from A to Z. So, you see, a sigil is a symbol that is meant to embody a complete idea. It's meant to denote the entirety of a thing, a "summing up" of that thing's attributes.

Ceremonial magicians were known to use sigils representing certain spiritual entities—demons, archangels, etc.—in order to gain control over them. Employing the sigil or symbolic representation of that entity was like calling its true name and binding its whole being, which was thought to be an irresistible force to that spirit. The sigil or symbol would be drawn, with focused will, by the magician inside of a sacred circle, and through ritual, the entity would be summoned to that place and charged by the magician to do his bidding.

So you see, sigils are very powerful. And you can create a sigil to represent your own intentions.

Grant Morrison is a well-known Scottish comic book writer, who also happens to be an occultist and chaos magician. He has put forth one way of creating a sigil that involves reducing your "intention sentence" to a symbol. The process involves reducing the sentence to its most refined degree. It must be stated as though the desired outcome is already a reality. It must be as concise as possible, and it must state the outcome, not as a desire ("I want") but as an existing fact. Imagine the future you, having already manifested the outcome, calling back to the pre-sigil you and expounding on the delights of the reality that exists after having manifested this outcome.

Then, take that sentence and remove all the vowels and repeated consonants. Next, take the remaining consonants and draw them into a symbol that represents your desire. There are no real rules for how this is done. The letters may overlap and overlay one another. The letters may be printed or written in script. You may stylize them to fit a theme.

Your creativity is part of the process for making your sigil a powerful symbol. Keep working to reduce yours, until you have a symbol that looks magickal to you. There may not even be a recognizable letter by the time you're done. Just keep refining and create something that is artistic, beautiful, and represents the idea that you desire.

This is the kind of intention that I drew on the back of that goddess picture in my mojo bag.

Charging a Sigil

Now, there are many ways to charge up a sigil. The creation of it is a big part of its charging. As you refine and redraw the image, you are placing your energy into it. With each stroke of your pen, as you reduce and concentrate the image, you are adding power to it.

Then, the sigil is meant to be "set" to its task in some significant way. I charged my sigil in the mojo bag, along with all of its other contents, by dancing ecstatically with it. At the height of the emotion, look at the sigil and, with your concentrated will, put that deep emotion into the sigil while visualizing your outcome.

Some advocate holding the intention and the symbol in your mind while you meditate or drop into a trance state in an effort to "push" the idea through the astral or etheric and then into the material realm.

Grant Morrison is famous for creating a sigil intended to boost the sales of his self-owned comic franchise *The Invisibles* and asking his readers and fans to masturbate while thinking of the symbol to charge it with their collective energy. At the moment of orgasm, they were to focus on the sigil and the intention. So, masturbation is a widely accepted way to charge your sigil.

The idea is to put your personal energy into it. Sing to it. Blow your breath into it to give it life. Take it with you on your workout until you reach runner's high. It's up to you and your intention. But know that this is a powerful and effective form of magic that will fire up your intended outcome. So make use of this tool.

Now that you have a bit of background and insight, let's get those spell-casting hands dirty and get right into it!

CAST A SPELL

Create a mojo bag spell with the intent of your own creativity and your successful alchemical transmutation!

Do your research and work with a spiritual entity that represents the kind of creativity that you need. If you have a very artistic ancestor, go with that. You could also work with Mercury, the planetary deity and god of communication. When writing, I work with Athena as the "weaver." But get a handle on your message and your desired outcome, and then choose a spirit to work with you. If you plan to sculpt Your Fairytale out of clay, then you may want to work with an earth deity. If you plan to tell a tale that involves myths of the indigenous people of the land where you live, then work with the land spirits. Do your homework and make it personal.

In choosing the mojo bag itself, as well as the items that will be put into it, remember to research the correspondences, but also, please, use your own intuition and your own ideas about the symbolism of the objects. That is what matters most. In western culture, the color white represents purity, but perhaps in your mind, culture, or understanding, black and the pure potentiality of the void is more appropriate. *Feel* your way into this spell. It will serve you well.

The ritual should also come from your heart and your understanding of what you want from this practice. Your sincerity and desire are infinitely more important to this work than the actions and steps themselves. Think on it, make offerings, meditate. Create the ritual that is right for you. No one will tell you that it's wrong, especially when your intended outcome manifests.

How you choose to use the mojo bag after it's created and charged is, again, up to you. My suggestion would be to keep it on an altar in your sacred space, where you work on Storytelling Alchemy. But you may also choose to keep it on your person or in your purse or pocket. Again, feel your way in it, and that will be the right choice.

Finally, take notice of any changes that take place in accordance with your spell's intent. Record your experience and any synchronous events in your journal.

SYNCHRONICITY

In an earlier chapter, I mentioned synchronicities. Synchronicities are those connections—or what some might term coincidences—that have significance and meaning for us. The synchronicity that Carl Jung frequently used as an example was when a female patient was telling him about a dream in which she'd been given a golden scarab. While she was still discussing the details of the dream, a beetle of the local variety most resembling the golden scarab flew in through the window. These two seemingly unconnected events—the woman's retelling of her dream and the beetle entering the room—not only happened simultaneously, but were connected in meaning.

Synchronicities are meaningful coincidences that apparently have no causal connection we can discern. Jung theorized that such connections were the inspiration for the beliefs of the ancients in concepts such as the Law of Contagion and the Law of Similarity.

A recent synchronous experience of my own is another example. My daughter is in her mid-twenties and in a stable relationship with a wonderful man. My significant other has a son of roughly the same age, also in a solid relationship. I would like to have grandchildren, and soon!

One morning I was told of a nifty texting system for an art museum. You could text to a certain number with "Send me [fill in the blank]," and the program developed by the museum's curators would reply to your text with an image of something on display in their galleries corresponding to your request. I was having fun requesting a few different things and finally texted, "Send me grand-children." A lovely image of a sleeping baby appeared and I was for the moment satisfied. Exactly nine minutes later—hmm, could that correlate to the human gestation period of nine months?—my signif-icant other sent me a text stating that he was going to be a grandpa.

To me, these occurrences are proof that my magick is working in the world. They are always a delight to recognize and still bring me a thrill, even though their frequency is so high that I could view them as commonplace in my life at this point. I do believe that this is because of practices like the ones described here in Storytelling Alchemy and my consistent use of magick. The power that these things produce is cumulative.

In this sense, I do believe that synchronicities *do* have causal connections, but science has not yet been able to show the links of these causations. Jung theorized this as well. He said that the indi-vidual psyche cannot be said to be localized—or in other words, that a person's thoughts *can* influence occurrences in the world and that even time may be relative to the psyche. Was my text message precognitive or causal? I don't know. But these are great ideas to contemplate.

MAGICKAL BEING EXERCISE

Perform your awareness, gratitude, and offering ritual in your sacred space. Still your mind and become aware of some instances of synchronicity in your life. Allow yourself to imagine, even if just for the moment, that they were indications that you are a magickal being with powers to make things happen in the world. Play out the idea that you may have been the driving factor in those synchronistic events. Spend a few minutes meditating on that idea and then write down your impressions. Try to hold the belief that you are a powerful and magickal being in your mind for the rest of the week.

In addition to this reflection, pay attention to synchronous events that may show you that the magick you've performed with your mojo bag is working. Record these impressions as they arise.

It is very important to acknowledge and express gratitude when you notice that your magick is working. So whenever you see these synchronicities in relation to the magick you've performed, make sure you give that gratitude and acknowledgment in the moment, and make sure that you address that again in your regular offerings to spirits and deity. Also, keep a record of them in your journal.

This will help to solidify in your mind that you are a powerful, magickal being. It will also add strength to future spells.

HYPERSIGILS

As I've said before, magick is cumulative and it involves both the conscious and unconscious mind. Your work in Storytelling Alchemy is part of the process of uniting those two powerful aspects of your Will. So, as you perform this rather epic work of transforming the SYTY into Your Fairytale, you will be creating what is known as a hypersigil.

We've discussed a bit of general magick, and we've discussed sigils. Now what on earth is a hypersigil?

The term *hypersigil* was coined by Grant Morrison, comic book creator and chaos magician. Morrison wrote about hypersigils or supersigils, among other things, in a piece called "POP MAGIC!" which appears in *Book of Lies: The Disinformation Guide to Magick and the Occult*.[2]

Morrison describes a hypersigil as "a sigil extended through the fourth dimension" of time. While a sigil is a single still image, a hypersigil involves time frames, characterization, and a plot. It represents an idea in the same way that a sigil does, but on a much grander scale. It is a whole story, perhaps a series of stories, ongoing and rich in the symbols that make magick powerful.

Morrison has said his comic series *The Invisibles* is a hypersigil. In a talk he gave at the 2000 Disinfo Convention at the Hammerstein Ballroom in New York City, he claimed that all of the trials and experiences of the character representing him in the series manifested in his real life. His hypersigil worked almost too well. He spoke of how he included a female love interest character in the series and, shortly after writing it, began to meet women who matched the description. At one point he ended up in the hospital with two collapsed lungs, closely mimicking a scenario he wrote for his character. After that, he

---

2. *Book of Lies: The Disinformation Guide to Magick and the Occult*, edited by Richard Metzger.

decided to be kinder and give his character some more positive out-comes! During the talk, Morrison keeps repeating, "It works! And everyone can do it!" This was a work of magick that has the ability to restructure reality.

But *how* does it work? No one really knows. Morrison encourages lots of experimentation and practice. Only in this way will we refine the how of magickal workings. There are theories, which are not much more than guesses, really, based on differing belief systems.

Those who believe that there are separate, autonomous spiritual entities around us may put forth that the work is like prayer and, if done well, may be smiled upon by the gods who bring about the desired outcome. Some folks have a perception of the universe containing a kind of vast energy that is malleable through our thoughts and words. These folks would believe that magick is a way of focusing those words to a fine point, which is more effective at creating the change we want than the way the average person thinks. Finally, there are those who believe that the work of magick is purely psychological. The changes made exist only in the mind of the practitioner. Nevertheless, those changes in the mind and psyche cause the person's perspective and behavior to shift, eventually leading to the desired outcome.

In the end, if it works, does it matter which of the theories is true, or even whether there is some other explanation? If spellcraft creates the situations we want in our lives, who cares if you believe it to be "magick" or "natural law" or "psychology?" The end result is the same.

The stories produced with Storytelling Alchemy are hypersigils. Your Fairytale will take time and much energy and intention to create, and it may encompass real epochs of your life. It may cover mere moments or decades, but Your Fairytale is an epoch, nonetheless, as it depicts a foundational or significant experience in your life. Your

Fairytales are not single-intention symbols, but whole stories. Your Fairytale is a magickal spell that has the power to transform your life, as well as your perception of your life.

Write the *person you want to be* into your own character in the story and become that. *That* is the power of this practice. I will guide you through the process of creating the winning scenario that will embed your character's triumph deep into your psyche and bring lasting change.

In the next chapter, you'll learn some more of my personal stories and spells. I'll also share how those stories and spells transformed the way I think about my past and helped me form my own future. Then we'll explore some examples to help inspire you and move you forward.

CHAPTER 9

HOW IT WORKED FOR ME

This chapter is about me. Within these pages you will see how I came to the practice of Storytelling Alchemy and how I've changed because of it. I'll provide some examples of my own writing for inspiration and to give you an idea of what is possible for you to explore in your own healing journey.

I've enjoyed writing fiction and poetry since I was a child. For the most part, I didn't know where the ideas came from, and I didn't care. There was a simple joy in the creative process for me, and there still is!

It wasn't until I was older that I began to have an inkling of the metaphors I was creating with my fiction and poetry. Of course, the inspiration came from my life. It came from the things that moved me to emotion. I started to realize that the things I wrote about were helping me to work out the issues I was facing.

It was then that I began to write stories with more purpose, consciously trying to find understanding for my challenges.

When I realized, in my exploration of the occult and witchcraft, that I could consciously create my own life, I began to write differently. I wrote stories, intending to change my world. I wrote stories that might re-create my reality.

RUNNING WITH THE WOLVES

One of my first forays into using my words and stories to re-create reality came in an effort to try to change others.

I was a senior member of a coven and believed that the dynamic of the group was corrupted and the leader was not expressing the necessary requirements to save the group.

In truth, I was a part of a fledgling coven that was experiencing the usual growing pains of learning to be together, to manifest as a group, and to manage a large community of followers.

There was, needfully, a hierarchy in our ranks, and there were some rules for how gatherings and rituals would be performed and which members should attend.

During this time, there seemed to be a great deal of dissent between members and so much conflict. To me the trouble seemed to stem from a misunderstanding of what leadership and membership meant. Some of the leaders saw their roles as superior to those of the followers. But my understanding of leadership was to be in service to the coven members. We were not there to rule or to move the group in any particular direction, but to serve and to determine what was needed by the congregation and create that.

There began to be an atmosphere of exclusion based on "rank," which truly bothered me. My level of training in this particular wiccan tradition in no way indicated my level of spirituality or enlightenment, although some of our members seemed to be acting as if that were the case.

I began to wonder if there could be a way for me to convey my feelings about this to the group without overstepping the bounds of my position as a dedicant to the high priestess.

At that time in our coven it was the practice to share ritual duties. The elders or founders would trade off the tasks of facilitating ritual. At the same time I was very interested in the idea of story *as* ritual and storytelling being a transformative process.

My turn to facilitate a full moon ritual was approaching in January, which our coven, in our tradition, saw as the "Wolf Moon."

I had been researching the dynamics of wolf packs and decided to use this opportunity to convey a message to the group that might help to clarify the roles of all members.

I had learned of a documentary done by PBS about the Yellowstone Druid wolf pack. I watched the series and created my dramatization from that story. My hope was to teach the members of our community why hierarchy was needed but, perhaps more importantly, to show the elders that leadership was meant to be a service and not an honor or exaltation of status.

I devised a ritual where the participants were encouraged to behave as children being treated to a bedtime story. I encouraged the participants to wear pajamas and bring pillows and stuffed animals. The cakes and ale portion of the ceremony consisted of milk and cookies. I really tried to cultivate that atmosphere of childlike wonder at storytime. I wanted to eliminate resistance and defensiveness that way. I was instead trying to create an atmosphere of openness and suspension of disbelief. I wanted our congregation to be as children, listening to a story, rather than members of a spiritual congregation following a sermon.

This was my first foray into transformational storytelling, and it actually worked quite beautifully. Many things changed after this ritual. However, most of the change manifested in me, personally . . . not so much in those I was trying to teach.

Here is the story I told in that ritual:

Dana Darkfur—The Story of One Wolf's Journey

Dana Darkfur awoke to a feeling of warm and sticky jostling.

"EEEWW! Mom! I don't want a bath?!"

"There's a pack council meeting tonight, pup! And YOU are going to be clean for it!"

Dana made a futile attempt to break free. But her mother's relentless tongue kept on cleaning. She rolled her eyes, "Aww . . . council, schmouncil—what's the big deal?" Her mother's teeth pinched her haunches—"OWW!"

Her mother Aurora, a well-respected pack wolf, had raised litters before. She had seen the good that could come from being a cooperative pack member . . . and the ill that can come from not. She glared at Dana, her most difficult pup to date, and said, "Dana, one day you will understand the importance of being a member of the pack. It's Survival! It's Community! This is not just a way for grown-up wolves to make your young life miserable, you know! There are REASONS I teach you these things! You keep clean! You obey the elders! You never take from a kill of theirs without permission! If they say move your den, you move it! There are REASONS for all of it . . ."

Dana zoned out of the lecture that she'd heard many times. There was no escaping it. She reluctantly started helping with the bath, cleaning her muddy haunches. She began to daydream about hunting and playing with the other young wolves.

Soon she was free and out stalking a small weasel with her younger sister. Kyra was a pack wolf through and through. She ALWAYS obeyed, always followed the rules. Dana couldn't help feeling pity for Kyra . . . so much a carbon copy—she rolled her eyes.

The adults usually left the young ones to their stalking and play-hunting. It was good practice. And Kyra, being the good pack wolf, tried to emulate the hunting style of the older pack members. They took turns, she observed, stalking and chasing, until their prey was tired. Then they killed.

Dana, however, tried to hunt like a mountain lion or something. Kyra watched her chasing this little weasel. It was a speedy little critter! She knew not to interfere, because whenever Kyra tried to take a turn in their hunts, Dana would bite at her feet and chase her away! So she sat watching and let Dana chase. Dana ran this way and that after the weasel, which was very agile and kept changing directions and going around brush. It hid under one bush until Dana came close to one side and then burst out at full speed from the other side, setting off the chase again. This went on for quite a while until Kyra could see that both Dana and the weasel were breathing hard and slowing down.

She laughed a little and encouraged Dana. "Look, he's tired! Time for the kill! Get him!"

Dana said, "Don't think I won't!" and POUNCED . . . on nothing. The weasel had, well, weaseled out of her grasp. She chased some more . . . angry now . . . and POUNCED again!! . . . on nothing.

When the weasel escaped this time she rolled on her back and panted with her tongue hanging out. "I give up!" she said.

So Kyra stood up, trotted easily after the weasel, picked it up in her young but powerful jaws, and shook her head to break its neck. She raised her head high with the dead weasel dangling from her mouth, tossed a muffled, "Fanks fer wearin' it out fer me!" and pranced off happily, with Dana gaping after her as she went.

This was the way much of Dana's youth went. She always seemed a bit out of step, a little different from the others. She didn't really mind. She just didn't understand all this emphasis on the pack, the pack—always the pack.

The Council of Elders and the alpha male and female wolves of this pack known as the Druids were so revered, even feared. But it seemed to Dana that they only way they got to those positions was by being different, more aggressive. Sometimes their power came by killing a fellow pack member. The leadership changed paws so many times it was hard to keep track. This was a contentious group, fighting all the time.

Aurora had told Dana of a time in her own youth when the Alpha wolves and the council were steady and strong for a long time. Under their reign the pack grew to large numbers with healthy litters each spring. It was a peaceful and prosperous time. Dana wondered what was different then. What did they do so right?

As she grew to maturity, Dana did learn some pack lessons. She learned how much easier it was to hunt with friends and to partake of a group kill, when you didn't have to be "The Star." She also learned **what** and **when** she was allowed to eat. Sometimes learning was deadly!

She recalled a time as a pup when she spent a week in the den with a wounded shoulder, her mother pacing and fretting over her, licking at the wound until she recovered. Dana had *tried to take a small piece of a kill that the alpha male had brought in. A hard lesson, but well learned.*

By the time Dana and her sister Kyra had reached mating age, Dana still didn't know the secret behind the strength of those elders her mother grew up with, but she knew the failure of this group. Rule was only gained by fear and death. She had a lot of friends who were, by turns, terrified into submission and then longing for overthrow. Dana's mother Aurora kept to the party line. "Pack life is pack life. Do what you're told. Keep your head down. Get fed." That was pretty much her mantra these days. But so often, to Dana, Aurora looked sad and worried.

"The Peace-time," her mother had told her, "was marked by real trust. The elders cared very much for their pack. They took their responsibility seriously. It had never been about Force. There was power, of course, but it had been tempered by Compassion. There was Honor, balanced by Humility." These stories seemed to Dana to be just that . . . stories. She had never seen a time like her mother described. To Dana, it was just fiction.

Aurora was still a young and healthy she-wolf, and the alpha males had mated with her on occasion. And this spring she was to birth a new litter from the alpha. She was cautiously happy. The pack seemed to be growing.

But the alpha female was not happy. Aurora threatened her place because she had not been able to bear pups this year. And one evening very close to the birthing time, Aurora lay in her den, exhausted from the early evening hunt. And Dana watched as Genna, the alpha female, burst into the den and dragged Aurora out, snarling and biting madly.

She was about to intervene when she was stopped by Kyra. "Are you crazy?! She's alpha!" So the two young she-wolves watched as their ailing and pregnant mother was torn to pieces by this vicious bitch.

Two decisions were made that day. Dana turned and walked slowly out of the Druid pack territory to become a lone wolf. And Kyra, no longer under the fair and watchful eye of Aurora, set her sights on the alpha position and began to plot her rise to the top.

Years passed. Dana was learning a new way now. She HAD to be the star of every kill. Sometimes she went hungry, but she was surviving. She learned not to leave scent or scat too close to the territories of other packs OR her former Druids. She was learning determination, over dependence. She was learning to shelter rather than socialize. It wasn't pack wisdom, but it was wisdom just the same. And she was learning to lead, rather than follow.

Dana kept a sharp ear on the boundaries of other packs. She had to listen, more so than follow scents, because wolf packs tended to mark their boundaries with howls back and forth between. Sometimes Dana was right in the middle. And on those nights sometimes a loneliness grew in her center and she would join the howling. But she dared not give it full voice, lest she be discovered. Dana was a tough wolf but certainly not tough enough to take on a whole pack. This much she knew.

One clear, bright, winter day, Dana was hunting an otter near a stream. She kept to smaller prey for the most part. There was only herself to feed. But this otter was proving a difficult kill. She would stalk, quiet and stealthy as could be, and just when she was ready to pounce, the thing would do a flip and land in the water with a splash. It seemed to be playing with her, mocking her! An otter mocking a WOLF! Not a very smart otter . . . then again, maybe she wasn't such a smart wolf.

A sudden SNAP of a branch behind her made her jump so high in the air that SHE fell in the water and ended up facing the shore. The black male wolf standing at the water's edge was snickering. She glowered at him, laying her ears down flat and baring her teeth. He didn't flinch or move away. If this was an alpha from another pack, she could be in trouble. But he didn't smell of a pack.

He gave in first. He sat on his haunches and dipped his head and nose down slightly. A gesture of friendliness. He meant her no harm. She relaxed—just a bit.

Finally, he turned away and started walking, but kept looking back at her. She was meant to follow. She was very curious now and pretty certain that he was lone, like her. So, she followed—at a distance. He brought her to a fresh kill. He had apparently brought down a young doe. Impressive. A good meal-sized section of meat was already missing. He bent his snout to the carcass and pushed a bit of meat toward her. Then he backed away to give her some space and sat down. She was very hungry . . .

Some distance away from this meeting of the minds, a fierce battle raged on in the Druid pack. Kyra's run for power was both ruthless and brutal. She would not tolerate any other pregnant females. And her killing spree left the Druids' numbers decimated. Now Kyra and the alpha female were the only two wolves who would bear pups in the spring. Kyra's determination doubled.

After the night's hunt, when the females were feeding, Kyra stepped up to take part before her turn. Genna had not taken her fill yet. This was forbidden by pack law, but Kyra refused to back down and the battle began. They circled one another, ears laid back and snarling. As they leapt at each other, fangs flashing, Kyra's fury was so great that she even wounded the alpha male when he tried to step in.

As alpha female, Kyra would continue her reign of terror on the other wolves. They lost hope as fear gripped the Druid pack.

Dana awoke in the early evening with her new mate, Shadow, by her side. They would begin their nightly hunt shortly, and as Dana gazed at the full moon, she felt the first quickening of life in her belly. Suddenly, a strange feeling came over her. It wasn't quite fear. It wasn't quite loneliness. But it was very like both of those.

As they hunted that night, Dana wondered how this would work in the spring when the pups arrived. Lone wolves with pups didn't do very well. There was no one to watch the little ones when they hunted, and the kills had to be larger to feed the whole family. Dana began to suspect that it was time to return to her pack. So, Dana and Shadow started listening for their howls.

They returned to the Druid pack very quietly, and they were welcomed by some of Dana's old friends. She was glad to see them, but they looked even more haggard and frightened than when she'd left. And when she asked about Kyra, she discovered why.

Her friends tried to convince her to leave. The fact that she was pregnant made her a target for Kyra. They told her she *couldn't imagine how fierce and cruel her sister had become. But Dana knew. She had seen fierce and cruel before.*

She stood up straight and looked each frightened wolf in the face as she spoke. "There was a Peace-time in this pack once. Some of your parents told you about it. My mother spoke of it often. The leaders were wise and merciful. They saw their position as responsibility, not power. They protected the young. They allowed the adolescents to grow strong and to have a say in the way things went. The leaders of the greatest Druid pack that ever was ruled with love and trust. Their only thoughts were for the pack, ever the pack—and not themselves and their own power. We can make that happen again. We MUST make that happen again. For our ancestors sake . . . and for our pups sakes. Please . . . all of you . . . you who remember . . . help me."

She turned and headed straight for the alpha den. Kyra had heard the commotion and was up and ready for her. The scent of another pregnant female had her already snarling. She attacked and somewhere in the midst of the bloody battle realized this was Dana. Kyra hesitated. Dana didn't waste the opportunity. In an instant her jaws clamped around her sister's throat and Kyra was on the ground, with Dana's paw holding her down. It would've been easy to kill her, but Dana waited patiently until Kyra's fury subsided and some of the tension left her body. Dana held her just a little longer—until the whole pack was gathered and all knew who had won this battle. Kyra began to tremble and whimper beneath her and this was the sign Dana had been waiting for. She would not kill her sister. Kyra would bear pups this spring—healthy ones—and there were few enough here.

Dana finally released her sister and gave her a space of a few feet. Kyra let out a low growl with her head down, which turned to a whine as she backed away to find a new den.

Dana, now rightfully the alpha female, would assemble a council of wise, compassionate wolves. This pack would be strong again.

She climbed the tall rocks, up and up as the moon rose in the sky. She pointed her snout skyward and let out a howl, full voiced and clear. Her pack-mates joined in, and the sound grew strong and resonant, transcendent. The howls rose up and enveloped her. The sound spiraled up and up around Dana and above her to the sky, toward the moon. It was the sound of a pack united, and it made them stronger. It made the rocks seem a little taller. It made the moon look more luminous. And it made the world a better place.

After I delivered this story at our coven's January Full Moon, things started to change, but not so much in the way I'd hoped. I didn't change anyone else's mind about the way things should be handled in our coven. I had, apparently, set in motion a chain of events that would make me a lone wolf, leading my own pack far away from the coven I knew.

Shortly after this ritual, I started my own group: not a coven, but a gathering of like-minded folk who met periodically for ritual and communion. It was a glorious and rewarding time for me, and I am grateful for all that I learned and the people that I met during that time.

I ran a small spiritual community for a few years from my home after this ritual. I always looked to the ideals of leadership and community that this story expounded for our group. We were happy and learned much from one another. We saw one another as equals, and it was a time of beautiful communion with other members of a spiritual community, very rewarding and very fulfilling.

That was my spiritual life. My personal life, however, was going through some profound changes.

A TRIP TO THE DEEP

I wrote the following piece during a particularly sorrowful time in my life. I had had my heart broken and had fallen into a depression that threatened to overtake me. I was not a child at the time. I was "old enough to know better." At least that's how I felt about it.

I had been divorced for some time. My ex-husband did not break my heart. Whatever love we once had seemed to die a slow, almost unnoticeable death. That's not what this part of my life was about.

Let me backtrack a little bit. I faced some pretty fierce challenges in my early life. I was abused and molested as a child. I was raped as a teenager and fell into alcoholism that lasted into my late twenties. But I had fought back from all of that. I had worked hard for recovery and for some spiritual balance. I had forged a great deal of peace for myself. And I prided myself on my resilience and my ability to choose happiness. I do still, but my understanding of that happiness is much more rounded and stable and whole today because of this story.

So, I was divorced for a number of years and then fell head-over-heels in love with a man, like I never had fallen before in my life. It was breathtaking and exhilarating and absolutely wonderful. Our relationship blossomed, and I was proud to be with him. He was wise and sober and intelligent and funny and kind and romantic and sweet, and he looked and sounded exactly like Sam Elliott! I know, right? Jackpot!

We struggled through a long-distance beginning to our relationship, and then he made plans to sell his house in California and move to my town in upstate New York. We were being smart about it. We decided that he should find his own place nearby and we would continue dating and enjoying each other and allow the relationship to progress naturally.

But things happened and housing deals fell through—or weren't pursued—and when it was time for him to move, he had no place of his own. So, I invited him to live with me. What was the harm? We were already deeply in love, right? Yeah, not so much.

It lasted for three more months after he moved in with me, and then he left. He moved back west, and I did not understand what happened. It seemed to me that he was simply disappointed in his choice and decided to abandon the whole idea.

He remained kind and knew I was heartbroken, and I turned into something of which I was not at all proud. I became that woman: the woman who begs a man to come back to her. The woman who cries, "Why don't you love me?" Yeah, that. (Let me include here the fact that I was raised by a strong, independent, single mom who was fond of the quote, "A woman without a man is like a fish without a bicycle.")

So, I was heartbroken *and* ashamed of the fact that I was heartbroken. "Sam Elliott" and I remained friends and spoke on the phone from time to time over the next year as I fell deeper and deeper into a self-loathing sadness that was consuming me. It was all I could do to get out of bed and go to work. It took monumental effort to provide my child with a modicum of care and parenting. And all the while, with every conversation I had with "Sam," I would ask the same questions, over and over: "Why didn't you love me?" or "Why couldn't you love me?"

My pain was threatening to bury me. Then, one day, through a series of "coincidences"—or synchronicities—I was reminded of my writing practice. First, I found a poem that I'd written years before while I was clearing off my desk. Then, while I was driving home I noticed a rock painted with a yin and yang symbol. This symbol of light and dark tells us that there is a balance to life and that dark takes up just as much space as light. And I understood that I'd been spending so much time being ashamed of feeling sad and maybe it was time to explore why I couldn't just allow myself to feel it, to just let the dark be. Of course, I was afraid that I would never find the light again, but that's ridiculous, really. The only constant is change.

When I returned home from that drive, I began to write and tried to explore my fear of the dark. Here is the poem I created during that time.

The Deep

Little Penelope Pickering Prim;
Would always smile; always grin;
You see, as she grew, she was taught by her dad;
That one must never, Ever be sad!

Little Penelope would always keep;
From falling down into that dark Deep!

"Danger," said Daddy, "is down in that Deep!
"Don't ever dare dive, down where things creep!"

The Deep doesn't Dream
The Deep doesn't Do
The Deep's only job—is to rob you of YOU!

Daddy's "Do Not's" quite frightened Miss Prim;
"How does one keep from the Deep?" she asked him.

"Sadness and sorrow will drag you down there.
The second you sense the slight sting of despair;
Stop it that instant! And think something Fair!"

Felicity Fast was her Father's Advice;
To keep from falling down deep where there's ice.

Penelope pondered, "Happiness then,
Is how to avoid that dark, creepy den!"

So EVER she tried to stay bright and cheery;
For fear she'd be taken by that Deep dreary!

So little Penelope Pickering Prim;
Went on with her life, avoiding the grim.
Her Happiness Hobby, she called this endeavor;
To always stay cheery, however, wherever!

All joyful things, Miss Prim would collect;
From bright-colored clothing to the perkiest pets!

"Happy ever after" ended all of her books!
And even her friends all held happy looks!

The Building of Bliss; The Making of Mirth;
Were, to Penelope, so full of worth!

The Deep doesn't Dream
The Deep doesn't Do
The Deep's only job—is to rob you of YOU!

And what better way to cultivate joy;
Than that beautiful day when she fell for a boy;

Love is the answer! Happiness to keep!
This is the Cure for that dreaded Deep!

So Penelope loved and loved so fair;
That joy and laughter filled the air!
She loved that dear darling who brought her such glee!
Until that dark day when that boy did flee.

The Deep doesn't Dream
The Deep doesn't Do
The Deep's only job—is to rob you of YOU!

Penelope's plan was a failure it seemed;
In all her heaped happiness—she never dreamed!
That the very thing that brought her such joy;
Could crash her down into that dark dreary void!

And down she did dive—down into that well;
In darkness and sadness and sorrow she'd dwell;
Her collection of happy bright colorful things;
Did nothing to stop her; did not give her wings.

All of those beautiful things out there;
Were no match at all for this kind of despair.

The Deep doesn't Dream
The Deep doesn't Do
The Deep's only job—is to rob you of YOU!

Penelope sank down deeper than deep;
Inside the darkness—her smile to sleep.

No longer resisting the pull of this dark;
She let herself fall—losing her spark.
No longer able her elation to keep;
Miss Prim had surrendered to the vast endless Deep.

Her tears drenched her soul, her wails ringing out;
Her sad cries of "Why?" echoed throughout.

"Why was I denied this love I SO Wanted??"
By this question, Miss Prim was terribly haunted.

Long did she stay in the grip of the Deep;
Long did she linger—longing for sleep.

The Deep doesn't Dream
The Deep doesn't Do
The Deep's only job—is to rob you of YOU!

Till one day Penelope Pickering Prim;
Having lost her fear of the dark and the grim;
Looked all 'round this dread place called Deep
To see all those things she was warned did creep.

Darkness and dim, little light did shine;
But a little she could see . . . a little at a time.
Some creeping she heard at the edge of the light;
Some breath of foulness, just out of sight.

The Deep doesn't Dream
The Deep doesn't Do
The Deep's only job—is to rob you of YOU!

Miss Prim then gathered her courage to stand;
And stood there, just looking, then reached out a hand.

Her fingers touched something so smooth and so cool;
She moved closer to it—so not to be fooled;
Glass was this feeling—large flat and straight;
She stood there before it to patiently wait;

When her eyes were adjusted and light came at last;
She saw her reflection in this great dark glass.

She looked in those eyes so hollow and sad;
And once again asked that question she had;
"Why was that love I wanted so bad;
Taken from me? It took all I had!!"

The Deep doesn't Dream
The Deep doesn't Do
The Deep's only job—is to rob you of YOU!

Through tears she could see a change in the glass.
Her image grew radiant, bright at last.

A smile of serenity graced those lips.
The answer that vision gave was just this:

"All of those things of happiness bright;
All joyful possessions out there;
Were not what you needed to keep you in light;
For one day we ALL are laid bare."

To the heart she pointed, the smile never waning;
As this beauty of brilliance went on explaining.

"It's here that your light exists—always has!
It's here where your sought Love resides.
Within you, Miss Prim, are treasures that last;
At your center—where ALL love abides."

And the moment the finger touched her heart;
Penelope gasped with a twitch and a start!
A bright point of light sparkled brilliantly there;
Then flourished to fill her whole everywhere!

This light held a feeling, down deep in her soul;
That feeling was Love—vast and old.
It filled her whole being—drying her tears;
Then lighted the place she had been in for years.

No dreary cave did that brightness Light;
But her very own home; all tidy and right!
Penelope wondered, "How can this be?
All along the darkness was inside of me?"

The dark glass reflection then spoke one more time;
"It is true I am yours and you, dear, are mine;
You've found your way to the darkness and back;
And now Penelope, there is nothing you lack."

The Deep doesn't Dream
The Deep doesn't Do
The Deep's only job—is to bring you to YOU!

Now you've read the poem in its entirety, as though it just fell out of me, intact and exactly as is. But that is not how it happened.

This was the work of quite a few weeks. And over that time, I was still struggling. The start of the poem was my exploration of why I was so disdainful and fearful of depression, of my own sadness. The poem took many different turns and was changed several times over the course of the weeks.

During this time, I also began to make daily offerings. I decided that I was in need of compassion—but a certain kind of compassion. I chose to work with Kali, a Hindu goddess with fearsome iconography. She is usually depicted as blue-skinned, but this is meant to represent the deepest black. She is frequently portrayed with wide eyes and her tongue sticking out. She wears a necklace of skulls and a skirt of bones. In one hand she holds a large blade and, in another, the severed and bloody head of a demon.

About now, you're wondering where the compassion is, aren't you? Kali's frightening depictions are misleading, because she brings liberation from shadow, which is the highest form of compassion. Kali is a revealer of personal truth. The goddess of tough love, Kali is in your face but on your side. She provides the courage to face the truth and also to release yourself from the false self—the ego.

I knew that what I was trying to do was to make some unconscious and false belief conscious so that I could confront it and heal. This was why I chose to make an altar to Kali and to make daily offerings to her.

All the while, I was examining those things that brought me to this place. I looked at my mother's disdain for women who lost themselves over their love lives. I looked at how that affected me. I looked at my own fear of falling back into the darkness of my youth. I had to take a good, hard look at the egoic part of my pride over having "recovered" from my childhood difficulties. I realized I had an attitude that said, "I don't get depressed! I'm all better now! I'm finished with that!" Ha!

When I arrived at the part of the poem that talks about losing the love she wanted, I got stuck. Big-time stuck! This was the hurt I was denying myself. This was the part I truly didn't understand. I spent days and days sobbing great big tears, fussing and fussing over the *why* of it all. How could he leave after all that we'd shared? And why wouldn't he admit that he didn't love me? This dialogue went on in my head with a desperate, whiny, sickening, urgency for *weeks*!

I would return to the poem and try to work something out. But it just wouldn't come.

One day, I had one more conversation with "Sam" where I, once again, tearfully begged for the answer to my question, "Why didn't you love me?" And, once again, he insisted that he *did* love me. I finally ended the conversation, unsatisfied with his answer. I left the house and was driving to get my daughter who had been staying with her dad—which, of course, was why I had all that time to cry and sob!—and the dialogue in my head changed a bit.

Suddenly it was as if a different voice had joined in—a calmer, wiser one. And as that giant tearful *"Why didn't he love me?"* passed through my head one more time, the voice, calm, loving, reasonable, said, "You're asking the wrong question . . . of the wrong person." It stopped me and caught my breath.

I accepted this statement as Truth—which, of course, it was—and I said to myself, "Okay, my first guess is that the person I should be asking instead of *him* is *me*. But what is the right question?" And then it hit me. It emerged from my subconscious like a breaching whale rising from the surface of the ocean: "Why do you need him to tell you he didn't love you?" And the answer came instantly. In that calm, wise voice, which I now recognized as my own, I heard, "Because I have a deeply held belief that I can't be loved."

I still remember so vividly exactly where I was at that moment. I was crossing over this little wooden bridge next to a church down the winding, rural road on which I lived. And in that moment, I felt love—*all* the love. I felt love like the brightest point of light in the whole universe, and it came from nowhere else but inside of me at the very center of my being. It felt as though I were literally being filled with light. It made me understand that this deeply held belief that I had had, that said I couldn't be loved, was *false* and was, in fact, ridiculous! How could I not be lovable when I *am* nothing but *love*?! That warmth and golden glow filled my entire being exactly like that bright spark that brought Penelope out of the Deep.

I went home, finished the poem, and put it away. And today, when I think of that time in my life, I smile. I smile about falling in love. I smile about the relationship. I smile about its ending. And I feel good about it.

And that, my friends, is Alchemical Transmutation—lead to gold, baby!

At this point in my life, I was still perfecting the techniques laid out in this book. But that writing showed me, like no other, how powerful this practice can be. That was precisely when I started to want to share this information with others and when Storytelling Alchemy was born.

You see, when we go on that Hero's Journey and we win out, slay the dragon, and get his hoard of gold, it is our duty to take those riches and return them to the place from whence we came. We have an obligation to share the treasure with those who are still seeking.

This practice of Storytelling Alchemy for healing, by the way, is not a one-time thing. I call it a practice because it needs to be done ritually. Every time I teach this course in a workshop, I write another story. Some have been epic tales of lifelong struggles and some have been about my fear of the dentist. Seriously, there's no end to what you can do with this tool.

IN THE DENTIST'S CHAIR

Now I'll share with you, dear reader, a more recent fairytale I've written with regard to my odontophobia or fear of the dentist. I've always had trouble with my teeth. I believe that good dental hygiene helps, but there must be a genetic factor as well because even as a young child I was meticulous about dental hygiene because I was told it would keep me out of the dentist's chair and I was terrified of the dentist. Unfortunately, I've spent many, many hours in the dentist's chair despite having good habits.

I had recently come from a dental checkup visit that brought me to tears. The prognosis was so bad, and the treatment so expensive and frightening for me that I left the dentist's office in a near panic. I did not go back.

A few weeks later I was teaching my Transformational Storytelling workshop and decided to use that incident and my lifelong fear as my inspiration for the tale I would write during that class. So, here is the story of Sarah of Dentalia.

Sarah of Dentalia

In a land called Dentalia, in a time not so long ago, there lived a little girl named Sarah, who was about to lose her first tooth. This was a very exciting thing, and Sarah was impatient for the arrival of the Tooth Fairy. In Dentalia, the Tooth Fairy brought magickal gifts for teeth left under pillows. It was always something different and unique and just right for the child.

One night, when her tooth was very loose indeed, Sarah fell asleep and dreamed of all things magickal and dreamed of meeting the beautiful Tooth Fairy. Most folks never saw her, but Sarah imagined her to be small and pink (perhaps lavender) and delicate and pretty and nice. In the middle of this lovely dream, Sarah was roughly shaken awake by a dark creature. It hovered heavily beside her bed. Its wings were dark and leathery. It was almost like a fat, round bat. The creature's teeth were large and white, but it didn't look like it was smiling. Sarah was frightened.

"I'm Zahnarzt! The Tooth Fairy! I received word about you and your teeth. I'm here to perform a pre-tooth-gathering inspection!"

Sarah was so shocked that her mouth dropped open and at that moment, Zahnarzt forced his way into her mouth and began tapping on her teeth with a small metal hammer! It was a horrible and frightening thing! He was making all kinds of exclamations and noises in there.

"Ugh! Terrible! – No, no, tsk tsk tsk! No good at all!"

He got out of Sarah's mouth, looked at her, and said, "These are no good! No need to collect them. You don't think the Tooth Fairy gives prizes for cavities do you?!"

Then Zahnarzt flew out of Sarah's window, shaking his head and grumbling, ". . . nothing worse than children with bad teeth. Terrible!" And he was gone.

Poor Sarah crumpled to her bed and wept, and at that very moment, her tooth fell out. She looked at it and sure enough, there was a tiny hole in the top. She cried even harder. Sarah decided not to put the tooth under her pillow, as was the custom. She was ashamed, so she found a box and put the tooth inside and then hid the box at the very back of her sock drawer.

Then she thought, "I'm going to take really good care of my teeth so that they'll be worthy next time." She was very conscientious. She drank lots of milk and brushed and brushed her teeth after every meal. And the next time that a tooth was loose, she thought she was ready.

But again, Zahnarzt appeared the night before her tooth fell out, and again, he tapped on her teeth with the hammer and this time it HURT! He told her again that her teeth were terrible and that it was her own fault.

Sarah cried, "But I brush all the time! I drink lots of milk!"

Zahnarzt shook his head. "You must be doing something wrong! These teeth are just bad!"

So once again Zahnarzt left Sarah crying, and when her tooth fell out, she hid it in the box in her drawer.

She tried even harder after that. Sarah stopped eating sweets altogether. She was brushing and rinsing her mouth five or six times a day now. But STILL, Zahnarzt would appear and make her teeth hurt and make her feel bad about them.

Eventually, all of Sarah's baby teeth collected in that shameful little box, and then, even her grown-up teeth started having problems.

Zahnarzt would show up at random times and invade her mouth. He always frightened her and made her feel ashamed. He said he was fixing her teeth with all his chiseling and hammering. It always hurt, and afterward, Sarah would cry herself to sleep with her mouth in terrible pain.

When her adult teeth started to fall out, Zahnarzt always said, "You just have bad teeth! More work must be done!"

And Sarah's life went on in this manner for many years. She always feared Zahnarzt's visits. One day, when Sarah had only a few teeth left, Zahnarzt once again scared her awake. He tried to act like he was helping her, but all Sarah knew from this creature was fear and pain. She finally became very angry. This time, when Zahnarzt tried to force his way into Sarah's mouth with his metal hammer, she bit down hard with her remaining teeth. He flew out just in time and hovered before her for a moment. Sarah screamed at him, "Go away! I don't care what you say anymore! You can't be the Tooth Fairy that I've heard of! All you've ever done is cause me pain and fear and expect me to thank you for it! And I have every reason to be afraid! Go away and never come back! I don't believe in you!"

And as soon as the words left her mouth, Zahnarzt vanished in a puff of dingy black smoke!

Sarah was so surprised and really began to wonder about something.

She reached into the sock drawer all the way to the back and pulled out that box. She looked out the window at the starry night and made a wish. Then she placed the whole box full of teeth under her pillow and went to sleep, smiling a nearly toothless smile.

Just before dawn, Sarah heard what sounded like bells. It was a small sound, and it gently woke her. When Sarah opened her eyes, there was a strange shimmering light in her room. And there, hovering ever so delicately in the air by Sarah's bed was a very pretty pure-white fairy. She was carrying a velvet bag that looked too big for her, but holding it didn't seem to take much effort on her part. Now THIS was more like it. Maybe she wasn't pink, but white made more sense anyway, didn't it?

The fairy pulled Sarah's box of teeth out of the bag she carried. "Sarah! I've been waiting and waiting for you to put a tooth under your pillow and now this! Why, oh why, did you wait so long?"

Sarah, who was understandably cautious, said, "Wait, who are you?"

"I'm Tanda, The Tooth Fairy!"

Sarah burst into tears and told Tanda all about Zahnarzt and how horrible he'd been all these years.

Tanda comforted her and said that she knew of Zahnarzt, and he wasn't a fairy but a tooth TROLL—a terrible creature! "I rarely ever meet his victims, because they go their whole lives and never place a tooth under their pillows. But you did something very brave. And you've given me all of these precious teeth!" She gazed at the cavity-filled teeth as though they were the richest treasure.

"But Zahnarzt told me my teeth were worthless and rotten and that he had to fix them!"

"Zahnarzt is a liar, and he cannot fix teeth at all!" Then she smiled brightly at Sarah and said, "But I can! Smile for me, Sarah!"

Sarah was ashamed of her smile but she tried, and what at first started as a simple showing of teeth (what few were left) slowly grew into a genuine smile.

Tanda produced a wand with one tiny, sparkling white tooth on the end and gently touched it to Sarah's mouth. And magically, all of her teeth appeared whole. They were shiny and strong and white and perfectly healthy. And from that day forward, there was not a brighter or more magickal smile to be found in the land of Dentalia!

This was actually a rather fun story to write. I've been practicing Storytelling Alchemy for quite some time now, and the subject matter tends to be less gravely traumatic. I tend to work on little things that bother me these days. And this was one of those things. But it did still spark quite a bit of emotion and also effected a great outcome.

As far as the magick that I perform these days when I practice Storytelling Alchemy, I tend to just do offerings, meditations, and depend on the magick of the story itself to manifest the desired change.

Whenever I finish writing a story, I recognize that I've created a new hypersigil, which needs to be "set" or "sent." I will generally perform a ritual that is in line with the intent of the story itself, but it invariably has to do with the emotion behind the story I was telling myself originally and the changing of that.

When I finished "Sarah of Dentalia," I entered my sacred space and brought with me the story, a mirror, some champagne, and a white candle that represented the tooth fairy.

I lit the candle and did my exercises to become present and meditative. I picked up the mirror and looked at my teeth. I took a really good look, opening my mouth, turning toward the light so I could see as much as possible. I smiled—or perhaps it was a grimace at first—into the mirror and beheld my full mouth of teeth.

Then I picked up my story and read it out loud. As I read, I allowed myself to remember all my hours in dentists' chairs and all my hard work in trying to take good care of my teeth. I remembered my disappointment and sadness each time the dentist would tell me that I had cavities and that my teeth were bad. I allowed the emotions to flow over me and into me and back into My Fairytale. My voice caught, and I choked the words out through tears.

When I reached the end of the story, I allowed the joy of it to enter me. I felt Sarah's triumph at finally being visited by the *real* tooth fairy. I felt Tanda's kindness and hope for me, and I felt Sarah's love for my own smile. At that moment, I spoke the title of My Fairytale three times, looking at the papers and the words: "Sarah of Dentalia, Sarah of Dentalia, Sarah of Dentalia." Then I blew out the candle and envisioned my new outcomes floating into the ether, delivering my message of transformation.

Since writing this story and sending out my hypersigil spell to the universe, I've become quite a bit more empowered in the dentistry department. I no longer allow my fear to keep me silent about my own dental care. I've looked into alternatives to extreme procedures like root canals, and I've sought out a kinder, gentler dental practice that helps me with the anxiety. I've discovered some dietary choices and mineral supplements that have improved my teeth. I even make my own toothpaste now!

So, there you have it, dear reader. I've provided you with a little insight into the crazy life of the author and some useful examples of how Storytelling Alchemy is done. I hope you were also entertained in the process. Next, we will dive into the work of writing Your Fairytale. I'm excited for you! Read on and let's get this project underway.

CHAPTER 10

TECHNIQUES:
MECHANICS + MAGICK = CREATION!

Now that you have gained some understanding of the history and importance of storytelling and a good idea of the things that make up a fairytale, as well as a couple of examples, let's discuss some techniques and ideas for moving forward.

If you've done the Memory Meditation in chapter 3, you have at least a couple of ideas for which SYTY that you'd like to make over. And it's still okay if you haven't made a final decision on that.

Let's discuss the actual writing process. Afterward, I have confidence that you will intuitively know which SYTY to use as your philosopher's stone.

Ahead of all of that, though, let's address the anxiety that some of you might be feeling about this endeavor. If you've ever experienced writer's block, or if you have some fear of getting this Truth down on paper—as I often do—turning to an outside genius can be very helpful.

I was inspired some time ago by a TED Talk called "Your Creative Genius," given by Elizabeth Gilbert, the author of *Eat, Pray, Love*. I highly recommend that you go find it and watch it. (All hail the Great Oracle Google!) It's about creativity, fear, and a lot of things to which anyone who has ever tried to write something can relate. Gilbert's talk also mentions the idea of a creative genius that dwells *outside* of the person and how it can allow for some space in which to lose your fear.

I've employed this idea as a way to relieve myself of some of the responsibility for the outcome of my writing. Earlier, I mentioned my storyteller figurine Alvarita, my truth-teller, and how she sits in my sacred space where I can see her. Each time I sit down to write, I ask her to give me the inspiration and the words that will allow me to give the right message to the world. I ask her for her genius. This invitation helps me to displace and alleviate anxiety about where the words will come from. Alvarita is like a muse for me. If I show up to do the work of writing, I want her to show up with her inspiration for it. She is the truth-teller, even when I'm writing fiction, because every bit of writing or artistry that you create, dear reader, is *your* Truth.

Especially when it's fiction, it's no longer the SYTY. Instead, it is your *Truth*. And Truth is powerful. Truth changes people, societies, and the world.

When I write, I'm hoping for publication. Your writings in this course are, first and foremost, for yourself, and you may not be experiencing hesitation in getting started. If that's the case, then just go for it. But if you're feeling the weight of trying to be perfect, or if you feel pressure about creating a really good story, try this technique of placing the "genius" outside of yourself and see if that helps.

STORY STRUCTURE

So what makes a good story? As boring as it sounds, we have to start with structure. All stories possess a beginning, middle, and end. (We will get to the creative, fun part! I promise!) This is known as a narrative structure. The story begins with the setup, by introducing the protagonist—that's you—and some of the characters, plus the theme and setting. A problem is presented.

The middle contains a conflict, where the characters' lives are changing, in turmoil, and being affected by the problem introduced in the setup.

Finally, the conflict comes to a head, and the characters must go to battle with it in order to come to a resolution.

This is also known as the three-act structure. Almost all good stories can be broken down into this format.

For an example let's look at *The Wizard of Oz*:

Act One: We meet Dorothy, her family, and most of the characters in one form or another. The setting and theme are introduced: a quiet little farming community in Kansas, where nothing much happens. Dorothy expresses a desire to find something else "over the rainbow." The problem arises in the form of a twister.

Act Two: Dorothy finds herself in a strange land with strange creatures and begins to confront the turmoil and trials of the Wicked Witch of the West, the fright of feeling lost, and the dangerous and eventful trek to the Emerald City and beyond.

Act Three: Dorothy, having overcome all the difficulties and triumphed over the evil witch and her own fear, is returned to her own bed and her loving family, with lessons learned and a newfound gratitude for life.

Some stories begin with the protagonist, as with *The Wizard of Oz*. The reader is drawn in either by a description of the hero or a situation in which she finds herself. Other times, some history is necessary in order to lay the groundwork for the big picture, and the story begins before we meet the protagonist.

We looked at the Hero's Journey earlier. This format was described and explored by the mythologist Joseph Campbell in his book *The Hero with a Thousand Faces*. According to Campbell, "A hero ventures forth from the world of common day into a region of supernatural wonder: fabulous forces are there encountered and

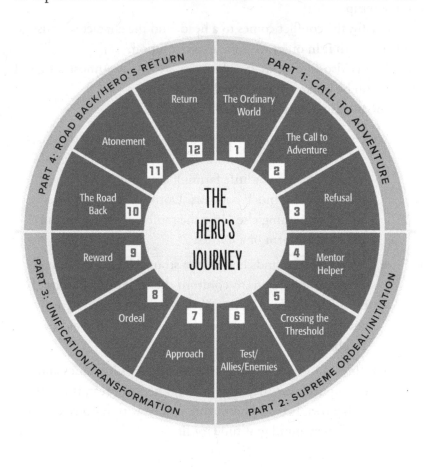

a decisive victory is won: the hero comes back from this mysterious adventure with the power to bestow boons on his fellow man."

The Hero's Journey begins in the ordinary world. We are introduced to the hero, who is often feeling out of place in his mundane existence. Frequently our hero has some ability or some quality that makes him stand out from others. Our hero may be depicted in the ordinary world, but something about him is not ordinary at all. He is special. The film *The Matrix* is a great example of the Hero's Journey. Keeping just to the four-part outline shown in the outermost circle above, this is how the story looks.

> The Call to Adventure: This can be an event or an individual prompting the hero on to some quest. Here, Neo receives mysterious messages about "The Matrix" and is instructed to follow the White Rabbit, leading him eventually to his meeting with Morpheus. He is invited to choose the red or the blue pill and the adventure begins.

> Supreme Ordeal/Initiation: In this phase of the journey, the hero must endure tremendous hardship and/or suffering. He must face his fears, learn the workings of the adventure world in which he finds himself, and overcome enormous odds. Neo is thrust into the real world and informed that everything he has come to believe is false. Neo finds a mentor in Morpheus and then must begin to accept this new reality, learn all that he can, and hone his skills. He is tested and challenged to increase his strength and discover his enemies.

> Unification/Transformation: Having been initiated, the hero now must venture off on his quest. He has been given some task to complete. Often this involves saving the world in some way. In our example, Neo has been charged with just

such a quest. Is he "The One" who will ultimately control and expose the Matrix to its masses of victims? Neo's ordeal brings him to the brink of death. But his valiant efforts and the love of the goddess (Trinity) bring him back to his reward. He has integrated all of his learning and has become whole (holy).

Road Back/Hero's Return: The hero has transformed into a being who has much to offer the ordinary world he left behind in part 1. He is now able to save the day. Neo returns to the Matrix with a message. He intends to bring truth to all of the inhabitants of the Matrix, thereby destroying it and setting its people free.

This is just one example of a formula you can consider as a framework for your story. I will, however, emphasize over and over that if you are ready to write or create and you have some clear ideas of where and how to begin, don't let the mechanics get in your way. Just begin your story and allow it to flow from you. If your heart is in it and you are not finding difficulty in getting started, then, please, write, create, and feel free to ignore these tips about story structure! You have total control over Your Fairytale. No one will grade it. It's yours. And because of that, you have total control over your alchemical transmutation.

ON THE NAMING OF NAMES

One of my favorite parts of writing fiction and inventing characters and places is naming them. In the Winged Wanderer story I will share with you at the end of this chapter, the characters even have dialogue about the importance and meaning of names.

Let me show you what I mean, using Sarah of Dentalia as an example. I chose the name Sarah for the main character (me) because of a song I remember called "Sarah Smile." It seemed right for the character who was ashamed of her own teeth. The land of Dentalia, of course, is a reference to the importance of teeth and the tooth fairy legend in this fairyland. Zahnarzt is the name I've given to the mean, mouth-invading, hurtful, shaming troll. It is the German word for dentist. I apologize to any dentists out there. This is just my experience and my phobia. The real tooth fairy in my story is Tanda—kind, helpful, magical, and sweet. She is named for the Dutch word for tooth, which is *tand*. Yes, I looked these things up. Yes, I wanted the meanings and correlations of those words in my story, even if I would be the only one who knew the meanings. Keep this in mind when naming your characters and your mystical locations.

PRACTICAL MATTERS

Now, let's get through a few practical matters.

Some people will be able to just begin writing, editing, and adding drama and characters as they go, and that's great!

Others, however, crave a plan. If you are one of those people, it may help you to begin with an outline. It should include just the basics of your story to give you a starting point and an understanding of your theme.

Here's an example:

Title: Winged Wanderer by Renée Damoiselle

Setting: An enchanted wood and an American suburbia

Characters:

Aletta: A mysterious elf-like creature charmed to look like a human girl.

Azzra: An elf who loves to frolic and has a good heart, even if a not-so-responsible character.

Constance: A lonely and loving woman who longs to be a mother.

Constance's husband: A cruel and bitter man.

The Scientist: a devious man, hell-bent on discovering secrets, with no care for the well-being of others.

Theme: Personal journey from self-doubt/self-loathing to joy, pride, and fulfillment.

The Story:

An apparent baby elfling is born to an irresponsible and unwilling elf and enchanted to look (sort of) like a human child and left on the doorstep of a human couple. She is named Aletta and grows up feeling as though she doesn't belong.

Her adoptive mother, Constance, is loving and protective, but Constance's husband is cruel and hurtful to Aletta, making her self-doubt worse.

Aletta suffers cruelty throughout her childhood for her unusual looks and is preyed upon by a scientist who suspects her true nature and would harm her to obtain "samples" to prove his theories.

Aletta wishes mightily to be something different. She prays for change, but when that change comes, her troubles seem even worse and she removes herself from the world of humans and ventures into the deep, enchanted forest. She has lost hope, but perhaps not for good.

OUTLINE EXERCISE

Go to your sacred space and perform your offerings and meditative ritual. Take up your journal and write down this type of an outline for several of the SYTY that you have in mind. You should have it narrowed down to three or four at this point. Make an outline for each one and review them in the meditative state of awareness that we've been practicing for all the exercises.

Allow each fairytale to develop a little further in your imagination. Record your feelings about each and whether you feel inclined to expand on the outlines. Some may inspire you; others may fall flat. Let this exercise help you decide which one should take on a larger life as Your Fairytale.

Choose the one SYTY that has the most meaning for you today. Remember, this is a practice. You may return to your other stories at any time you wish. So, choose the one that is the most relevant for you at this time in your life.

For the Indecisive

If you are having difficulty deciding which SYTY to use for Your Fairytale, read on for a little advice on this subject.

It's time. Please allow yourself to release your fears and embrace the adventure. Choosing the SYTY that hurts the most will be extremely cathartic and growth promoting, and it will move you far forward in your quest for enlightenment.

Choosing the SYTY that has the least emotional weight will whet your appetite for this practice and start you on a lifelong journey of a new kind of self-examination.

You see, dear indecisive reader, there is no wrong choice, except the choice to never begin.

I urge you to decide on one story even it if means you write them all down on a piece of paper, close your eyes, give the paper a few spins, and choose by blindly pointing. Decide and begin.

TAKING THE LEAP

When you've finally decided which SYTY that you'd like to turn into gold, it's time for one more Memory Meditation.

YOUR STORY EXERCISE

Go to your sacred writing space and perform your ritual of the senses, the same as every time before. Make sure that you have your journal and pen nearby. Become aware of, acknowledge, and give gratitude for the pleasing experience of the moment. As a reminder, here are the steps you should follow:

As you settle into your chair, acknowledge the comfort. Notice the feeling of the air on your skin. Close your eyes for a moment and give those sensations their due.

Then light your candle or incense or start your fragrance diffuser and take in the scent deeply. Appreciate that small pleasure.

Turn your awareness to the sound. Start your music or nature sounds and just take a brief few seconds to listen closely and be thankful for the beauty of the sound.

Now, if you've chosen to incorporate the sense of taste, take that bite or that sip and give it your full attention. Enjoy it deeply.

And give thanks in this present moment *for* this present moment. Recognize that this present moment is filled with pleasurable experience that you've created for yourself.

Take a deep breath, close your eyes, rest, and relax into your chair. Continue to breathe evenly.

As you relax and continue to breathe comfortably, understand that you exist in this safe, beautiful, sensual atmosphere for which you are grateful.

Continue to breathe and enjoy and be grateful.

When you feel peaceful, relaxed, and ready, then allow your mind to wander to that time of your past, the SYTY that you've chosen.

But step back from that scene in the following way: Observe it as if you are a fly on the wall. Try to eliminate judgment about what is happening. Float above the scenes and simply recall and view the action as it unfolds before you.

Remember that you are not being harmed anew. You are seated in your sacred space amid beauty, and you are safe.

Simply observe the action. Listen to the words spoken. Remember as clearly as you can and without judgment of good, bad, happy, sad, etc. Just see the events.

Allow the images to play out like a film.

When you feel as though the scene has played to its conclusion, breathe deeply and remember your impressions.

Allow yourself to recall that you are actually in your sacred writing space enjoying all these lovely sensations.

Rest in that for a moment. Then, when you feel ready, open your eyes and return to alertness.

Immediately write down your impressions of the memory in your journal. Be sure to record any new insights that you've gained from your objective observance. Write this log in the third person.

If you've followed the above instructions, you've remembered a thing that happened and it was not a happy thing. And now I'm encouraging you to make a fairytale out of it. So where's the happy ending? You and your intentions will create that happy ending and the empowerment that goes along with it.

The major part of the story may symbolically follow the terrible events of your past and will no doubt include the sadness, anger, and hurt involved. But your job in creating Your Fairytale is to change all that so that the story ends with your character in triumph.

How? There are a few techniques that you could use to make this happen.

For example, if your story lacks in motherly love and that is what you needed, bring in a new character to provide that to your own character. She may be a kindly fairy godmother or a wise old crone who is on your side and aids your outcome with love and magick.

Again, look to the archetypes of your story, and if there was an archetypal energy missing in your real life—like Mother, Father, Teacher, or Trusted Friend—include a character that embodies that for you and accept their love, kindness, wisdom, and support through the storybook you. Allow them to give you what was missing.

Perhaps the SYTY leaves you with the feeling that you should have done something differently. Perhaps you wish you'd had more courage. Perhaps you wish that you had said something that just didn't come out in the real world. Give your character whatever was needed; a warrior spirit, a superpower, more faith, more love, more perseverance. Put the right thing into the plotline to make the ending happy. Change the Story You Tell Yourself.

I had a student whose story involved a lot of pain relating to family relationships. She realized she was holding grudges that were unhealthy and hindering her in her life. Let's call her Olivia. Olivia portrayed her whole family as lovebirds. She recalled the early days when there was love, support, and nurturing among the members of the family. But they were beset by some trouble that made them forget who they were for a time, abandoning each other and acting in ways that were not at all loving.

Olivia turned her story around by making her own character the catalyst for her whole family's healing.

They all came back to their own loving nature and ability to heal. Soon they formed a school together where all kinds of birds would come to learn how to heal themselves and others.

This was a beautiful reconciliation of the family in Olivia's understanding. When she cast the family as lovebirds, she chose to see that the true nature of her family members was love and not the hurt that she had experienced. In reconciling them in her story, she found forgiveness and freedom.

Trust that you can do the same. The tips that I've given here are just to give you some ideas about how you might make changes. But, trust me: once you begin to tell the tale, your own ideas of how to "fix" the hurt will arise. Believe the ideas that come to you. Allow them to play out and get them all on the page. Once it's done, review the story and see if you want to change anything. Allow the words to flow.

ADDING THE MAGICK

Now that you've been given some tips about the mechanics, it's time for a little more on magick!

I believe in something I like to call cumulative magick. I've been known to say that everything counts. Throughout this book you've been performing magick, learning about correspondences, meditating, and delving deep into your history and the history of storytelling. And presumably, you've been doing all of that in your sacred space.

Hopefully you've been learning more about yourself. To me, one of the most important keys to good magick—and by "good" I mean it works—is to "know thyself," as Socrates told us.

We've talked about making the unconscious conscious, and that is a big part of the process. Once your unconscious is on your side in achieving your goal, it will happen. It's just a matter of time and persistence.

And here's the thing: it takes work and time, and you are never done learning about yourself or about how your magick works. You will accomplish the transformation we are talking about in this book if you do all the work here. But on the heels of that will come another goal and another unconscious belief that must be brought to light and dealt with.

Your sacred space, by the way, will help you in this endeavor. It accumulates the energy of the events that take place, like ritual, meditation, and magickal workings. It builds a power of its own. This is why I encouraged you to create it and keep it clean and beautiful while performing all of your work there. These actions add power and momentum to your journey toward your goal.

Sometimes the spell doesn't work the first time you do it. So you devise a new one and come at the issue from another angle. Or you simply refine the one you did and try again. You see, we don't know the science behind the magick yet. And that leaves spellcraft in the realm of art rather than science.

Each practitioner must work to perfect their power and spellcraft over time and through frequent practice. Mistakes will be made. That's the nature of the beast. However, the good news is everything counts! If you are working toward a goal, every bit of self-knowledge you gain, every spell you try, every moment of meditation on the outcome moves you closer to achieving it. So there really are no mistakes; there is only learning. And you'll keep improving, not just as a magickal practitioner, but as a person.

With magick on your side, you can accomplish your goals more quickly and even with more fun—especially when you get good at it.

And how do you know you're getting good? Your spells begin to work, and then they begin to work faster. Soon, your thoughts and words become more focused than they've ever been, and even the things that you say begin to manifest.

You'll notice synchronicities and connections. And this will begin to happen more and more frequently. Remember that a synchronicity is a series of events or so-called coincidences that seem to have no causal connection, but have meaning for the person who experiences them. *Meaning* is the key word here. I believe that's why we're here: to bring meaning to our lives and the lives of others. And when synchronous and serendipitous events are happening in your life almost every day, you are immersed in meaning. It's wonderful to live a life like that. You'll see! It makes the journey toward reaching that goal so much more rewarding and joyful.

TIPS FOR HONING YOUR PROCESS

The following are a few final tips before you really dive in and create Your Fairytale and hypersigil.

Now that you've gained some perspective with your meditations, studied story in some of its many manifestations, recorded your impressions, and prepared magickally, it's time to begin creating Your Fairytale.

As you've seen, stories can be told in many ways. I am a writer and that is what I know. But if your creative talents run to the visual arts or to music, then please feel free to create Your Fairytale in that way.

In teaching this workshop in person, I've encountered many different ways to manifest the desired outcome.

One student created a beautiful and textural collage of images to tell her story. It included drawings, photographs, stickers, glitter, tissue paper, paint, and her whole heart and mind. It was perfect *and* it helped her. She expressed great excitement about creating more like it to address other issues in her life.

Another student compiled a collection of music that told a story about her relationship with her father and her feeling of loss. She sang for us in the final class. There was not a dry eye in the group. And she told me that she could feel the healing begin.

What is powerful in this practice is what is, above all, powerful for *you*.

If you are a visual artist or a writer in another genre and you've grasped the concepts here and can incorporate them into your own medium, then, by all means, do that.

I've written about using the fairytale format because that is what has worked for me and I've seen it work for others. But your ideas are just as valid. If you plan to be brave, delve deep, and give it all of your honesty and sincerity and creativity, then go for it! The product that you create should have meaning for *you* above all else.

Make It Fun

Whether you plan to write or produce some kind of visual or auditory art, I want you to make it fun.

For your first writing session and beyond, if you choose, I want you to incorporate and have ready some items from your childhood. Specifically, get some construction paper, crayons, markers, paints, stickers, glitter, etc. You may want to draw a picture of the ogre in Your Fairytale. You may want to put a crown on the princess.

This is another way to incorporate that childlike wonder that is important to this process.

If there are creative tools that you love or loved as a child, have those at the ready. However you love to create and whatever brings you back to the joys of childhood, incorporate that into your writing sessions. You may never feel the need to use them, but knowing they are available to you will help.

For one of my writing sessions, I included a toy from my childhood known as Silly Sand. I found a recipe for making my own, as it was no longer available in stores. When I was a child, I used to build sand castles for hermit crabs with this dribbly, wet sand, and I always found it soothing and joyful and creative. That's the sensation we're going for here. Open your mind to your childhood joys and see what you come up with.

Freewriting

Every time you sit down to work on Your Fairytale, begin with some "freewriting." Approach your sacred space as usual. Still the mind, and appreciate your surroundings. Make an offering if you like. Open your journal and take up your pen. Now, simply begin writing. It doesn't matter what you write at this time. Just dump whatever is in your head onto the page. At first, the things that are in your mind—like the day you just had, the bills you need to pay, the chores that are waiting—will come out onto the page. Allow that. It will help to clear that clutter away, so that you can get to the real task at hand.

As you continue, you will find that more of Your Fairytale seeps into what you are writing. Allow that, too! When your mind becomes more focused on what you want to create and at the point when you feel inspired, end the freewriting session and get down to the business of creating Your Fairytale.

ONE FINAL EXAMPLE

Of the examples I've shared with you so far, one was a poem—a perfectly acceptable medium—and one was more of a traditional fairytale. This last one is a very typical fairytale as well.

When I wrote this story called "Winged Wanderer," I had decided to take on the larger issues in my life. I've mentioned earlier that I did not have an ideal childhood, as I'm sure is true of many of you. In this story, I tried to cover a large expanse of time in my life, from birth to my earlier mentioned recovery from the issues I perceived.

I will give you the highlights of the background story.

My birth mother, after some indecisiveness, gave me up for adoption. I've never thought ill of her for it. I felt it was a very unselfish thing to do. My adoptive mother was a wonderful, loving, and protective woman. Her name was Constance, and I've kept it so in this story to honor her.

My adoptive father was cruel and abusive and caused me much harm in my childhood.

In my adolescence, there was a stepfather figure who beat my mother and raped me when I tried to defend her.

In addition to all of these things—and in some ways, perhaps because of them—I always felt different and as though I did not fit in. I definitely had what is known as the Ugly Duckling syndrome. When I tackled this story, I was ready to be truly finished with all of that.

I had put most of the hurt behind me when I wrote this, but the process really helped me to come to a more complete understanding of those times in my life.

All of that darkness was, for me, like being in a chrysalis of sorts. This story and my magickal practice were the catalysts to opening that cocoon and emerging in flight.

I hope you enjoy this story and I can't wait for you to begin writing your own.

Winged Wanderer

A smallish pink fluff floated in the sunshine. It looked like a fluff of the sort upon which a child would make a wish as she blows on a dandelion. The fluff went turning and weaving through the air in a brilliant green field. It flew effortlessly toward the edge of the great, dark forest. It could be seen wafting into the shadows, occasionally set aglow by the rays of the sun that filtered through the canopy. The shadows began to swallow this tiny bit of flotsam as it delved deeper into the woods. It shone once more in the light and then vanished into the darkness.

A while later, deep in that very same wood, a plump and happy elf-ess lay sleeping and snoring in the hollow of her tree. A nearly empty bowl of berries sat by her bed and her smiling face was stained purple with the juices. Something tickled her nose and she awoke with a sneeze. As she sat up, a sudden, bright glow from the corner of her tree hollow caught her attention. As the light dimmed, a rustling sound was heard and then a tiny voice. "Ep! Aggle! Goo!" it said!

Azzra (for that was the name of this elf-ess) stood up and went cautiously to the corner to investigate. Wide-eyed, she stared at the elfling that had appeared there. "Oh, NO!" she cried. "I've gone and sneezed out a baby! Oh, NO, Oh, DEAR! What shall I DOOO?!"

She placed the elfling into a hollowed-out gourd and brought it to the meeting grove.

"What've you got there, Azzra?" cried the over elves.

"I've gone and sneezed a wee one!" Azzra exclaimed, in a rather angry tone.

"Oh, NO! Azzra! Not YOU!" they said. Azzra was a bit irresponsible—even for an elf.

Azzra held out the gourd containing the little elfling as if offering the child. The others backed away, frightened. It was bad luck to raise the elfling of another.

"You have to take care of it, Azzra! You must!" they told her.

Azzra's distress was quite obvious. "But . . . but . . . I've so much frolicking to dooo!" she whined and looked down at the elfling with concern.

Elves are not known for their parenting skills, you see.

Two of the other elves, trying to help, asked what Azzra would name the little bundle. Azzra looked even more distressed.

One of them offered, "Call it Al! That'll work!"

Azzra looked closely at the elfling and said, "NO! It's a girl!"

Another elf burst out, "Etta! Call her Etta!"

Azzra thought for a moment and said softly, "Aletta." (Somehow it sounded familiar as though it had been whispered to her while she slept.) "Aletta, that's her name!" And finally she smiled. And so did Aletta.

Azzra took Aletta home, resigned to taking care of the little elfling.

But after a few days, the task proved too difficult for her. "How is one supposed to survive for SOOO long without frolicking?!" She made a decision. There was a human couple who lived at the edge of the forest. So Azzra conjured a glamour on Aletta. Azzra breathed a pinkish hue over Aletta's green little body to resemble the skin of the humans. She waved her hands over Aletta's ears and hands and feet to make the points and claws less noticeable (especially to humans). Then Azzra placed the wee one in a basket suitable for carrying human babies. But then Aletta looked so tiny! So Azzra summoned all of her power to puff the little elfling bigger, until she almost filled the basket. The elf-ess called it good, stealthily placed the basket on the porch of the human couple, and turned to go back into the woods. She looked back once to see the delighted look on the face of the lady who opened the door and felt satisfied and went off to frolic with her elfin friends.

The human lady, upon finding Aletta's basket WAS delighted. "Look at this beautiful pink baby!" she said to her husband. "She's so cute, and looks so pink and healthy. Surely someone wants us to raise this girl as our daughter, since we've no children of our own. The gods have blessed us!"

The husband looked down at the child and scoffed. "It doesn't look that healthy to me! If the gods were good, they'd have sent us a good strong boy instead of this useless ugly girl!"

The lady, whose name was Constance, took the baby into her arms and cuddled her protectively, as if to shield the child from the harsh words. Then Constance saw that there was a leaf in the basket. The veins of the leaf appeared to spell out a word. For a moment the letters glowed golden against the green leaf. They spelled "Aletta." "That's what I'll call her," thought Constance. "Aletta is a pretty name."

Aletta had no memory of her elfin beginnings, but she did know she was different. Aletta would crawl into Constance's lap and look at her mother's lovely, pale pink skin and wonder why her own always seemed a little greenish. She loved to tell her mother "secrets." Mostly, they were whispered nonsense and babble. What Aletta REALLY wanted was to look at Constance's beautiful, small, round ears. When she looked at her own ears in the mirror, they always seemed so big and pointy. Aletta just felt different. But she knew her mother loved her, in spite of her weirdness . . . and maybe even because of it.

But whenever her father caught her looking in the mirror, he would twist her long thin fingers until they cracked loudly. He would stomp on her long thin toes until they were bloody. And he would pinch at her greenish skin until it was bruised purple and blue. Then he would leave Aletta on the ground crying and tell her to stop looking at her ugly reflection. He told her that she didn't belong. After her father went away, Aletta would run to her bed, where she'd built a little cave of

curtains, and she would hide and cry and feel all alone. Alone
. . . and ashamed of what she was . . . ugly . . . different.

Soon Aletta went to school and met other children. They
were just as cruel as her father—maybe worse. You see, glam-
ours don't work as well on children as they do on grown-ups.
They were better able to see her true nature, her green skin, her
pointy features. And they called her Troll. Little did they know
that they had the creature completely wrong! If they had dared
to mock an actual troll, there would be many little children
bones collecting under bridges!

Aletta would come home crying more days than not. She
would retreat to her curtain cave and wish so hard . . . wish
SO Hard that she would change! She didn't quite know what
to change TO—just "CHANGE, PLEASE!" she wished . . .
"to ANYTHING else!"

When Constance discovered that her husband was hurting
Aletta, she made him leave the home forever, so Aletta knew
that her mother loved her and wanted to protect her. But
afterward, her mother seemed different and unhappy and had
less time to be with Aletta. She would no longer let her whisper
her secrets and she was away from the home more and more.

Aletta was spending more and more time in her cave of
curtains, wishing for change. Then one morning she did notice
a change. Her body was covered in a light layer of pink fur!
The pink fur contrasted against her greenish skin, making it all
the more noticeable! "Oh, NO!" This was not the change she
wanted! Now, feeling even more freakish, she simply covered
herself up as much as possible, feeling more and more ashamed
and still wishing for a different life.

Then one day, Constance brought home another man. At
first the man was very nice to Aletta, and she liked him. Aletta

was becoming a young lady now and understood that her mother was lonely, so she was happy for Constance.

The man would always compliment Aletta and bring her little gifts, more so than he did for her mother. He said he wanted to be her friend. And Aletta's mother was happy to see someone treating her daughter well.

But the man had a secret. He was a scientist from a nearby laboratory! Now, not all scientists are mean or bad, but this one was cold and evil. He didn't care about elves OR people, he just wanted to be famous for proving that elves really exist. And he had his suspicions about Aletta. He'd heard the stories of what the schoolchildren had seen.

By this time, Aletta's pink fur had grown into a long thick coat that she was constantly trying to hide with more and more clothing. And one day, when she was looking disgustedly at her fur in her mirror, getting ready to cover up, the scientist burst into the room and saw! And in that moment the glamour faltered and the scientist saw Aletta the ELF! He violently grabbed her and wrestled her to the ground. Constance heard Aletta's cries and came running, but the scientist hit her so hard that she crumpled to the floor in a heap. This angered Aletta so much that instead of trying to escape she attacked the scientist, teeth and claws flying. But he was too big and strong, and he forced her down on the ground and tied her there. He wanted samples from a real elf for his experiments, so he cruelly pulled out chunks of her pink fur. He cut off the tip of one of her pointy ears and took her small clawed toe! All the while Aletta screamed and cried.

The scientist finally left, and Aletta cried and tended to her wounds for days and days. Her mother got better but was not the same. As Aletta healed, her fur was growing back quickly, thicker and longer than before! She was horrified! But somehow she also felt that the fur covering her body was protecting her in a way . . . pulling her away from the world she knew. She guessed maybe this was the change that she had prayed for.

Aletta and her mother were both so sad, and she knew that her mother became sadder every time she looked at her. So she decided to leave and go alone into the forest. She still didn't know what she was, but she knew she didn't belong in that home any longer.

So into the woods Aletta trekked. She wandered for a long time. She wandered without hope in the darkness of the forest. She didn't care what happened to her now. Her fur had grown long and full and covered her whole body. Only her green face and green, pointy ears were visible now, and Aletta just didn't care. As she went through the forest, day after day, week after week, twigs and leaves became stuck in her fur. It dragged on the ground and became very dirty and picked up pebbles and insects. Tangles and mats began to appear in the fur, and it lost its shine and was so filthy that it began to look more brown than pink. She looked down at herself with disgust and shame. Whenever another woodland creature was near, Aletta would hide, and she wondered how she could feel so ashamed but also not care at the same time. In fact, she cared so little and wandered for so long that she actually forgot her own name. Finally, she found a cave that reminded her of the curtain cave she'd built as a child. She decided to stay there.

She didn't need a bed on the cold, hard rocks, because her fur was so thick it cushioned and protected her. Aletta lay down and went to sleep, hoping that she would not wake up.

But she did wake up. And there was someone (something?)
standing in her cave, looking at her. Aletta started and sat up.
Staring at her, wide-eyed, was an old elf-ess. Aletta couldn't
believe her eyes. This lady looked the way she had looked before
the fur. Could this be what she was? But this lady had no fur,
only green skin and pointy ears. The elf-ess blinked and touched
Aletta's fur in disbelief. Aletta flinched and pulled away.

"Oh, I don't mean to hurt you! I'm a nice elf . . . the frol-
icking kind!" She smiled. "It's just, this fur . . . don't you think
it could be soooo pretty if you . . ., you know, did something
with it?"

It's true, this elf-ess was Azzra, from Aletta's long ago,
but neither one recognized the other. Aletta stayed quiet and
wary but let the elf-ess stay. And Azzra began to groom Aletta's
fur. She gently pulled out the twigs and leaves and bugs. She
brushed and brushed to take out the tangles and mats. Azzra
would go off to frolic from time to time, but she kept return-
ing to work on Aletta's fur. And after a time, when Azzra was
gone, sometimes Aletta would continue and brush and groom
her fur herself.

One day Azzra coaxed Aletta out of the cave to the stream
to wash. When they returned to the cave and Aletta looked
at her reflection in a puddle, she smiled for the first time
in forever. Azzra said, "See? You're beautiful! What is your
name?"

Aletta's smile faltered, "I don't know!" Azzra was disap-
pointed, but then brightened and said, "I'll call you pinky for
now, dear . . . but names are important, they all have mean-
ings, you know. I've learned a lot about names over the years."
She looked off wistfully into the distance for a moment. And
Aletta thought there was something sad in that look. "Anyway,

I bet that when we get your fur looking all beautiful and shiny and perfect, I bet THEN you will remember your name. And I bet it's really pretty too!"

So they continued each day to groom the fur a little more. The pretty pink color returned, and as the tangles went away, the shine returned. Aletta ventured out of the cave more and more and met other creatures in the forest. A unicorn offered some hair from its tail for Aletta to make a brush. The brownies scavenged a real mirror from the people world and brought it to her. The chipmunks would bring her flowers to put in her hair.

And one day, something magickal happened as Aletta gazed into her mirror, brushed her long, luxurious fur, and tucked a lovely purple flower by her ear. She looked at herself and loved, truly loved, her reflection for the first time ever. She gazed into the mirror and saw only the most beautiful, unique, pink-furred creature there ever was. And then, she remembered her name. She whispered "Aletta." And Azzra said, "What's that, dear?"

"ALETTA!" she said, "That's my name! You were right! I remember!"

Azzra looked in shock at this pink-furred creature that was once her very own elfling . . . and then, she understood.

She grabbed Aletta. "My dear child! Oh, now I get it! I didn't sneeze you, as elves sneeze out their young! You came to me on the breeze! You arrived through the open window on the wisps of the air and landed in the corner of my tree hollow!"

While all this babbling was going on, Aletta just stared, confused and shocked.

But Azzra continued, "You're not a human, my dear. And you're not an elf either!"

She turned Aletta toward the mirror again. "Look at your fur! It's starting to glow and sparkle and rise up!"

Aletta looked, and it was true. The fur was starting to rise up like some static charge was lifting it to the air. And it was sparkling AND glowing. And as this happened, her tiny body was revealed underneath. Aletta thought it was the most beautiful vision she had ever seen, and again, her love flowed to herself. And in that moment, the fur swirled and blurred and started to come together. Colors, so many colors, started to infuse the fur as it fused together and suddenly it all collected at her back and formed into WINGS!

Azzra said, "Aletta, I told you names were important! Aletta, my darling, means 'Winged Wanderer'! You were a tiny fluff that floated into my window, and I mistook you for my own elfin child. And then I gave you to humans, and you mistook yourself for human—but different. And now you know, my dear. Now you know."

She was a FAIRY! And she was beautiful beyond imagining! And she could fly! And oh, did she fly. In fact, she flew happily ever after.

And there you have several examples of My Fairytales. I hope that they've enlightened, inspired, and entertained. Remember to keep your mind and imagination open to the medium of telling a tale that resonates with you.

Because *you*, dear reader, are the driver of your life, and *only you*, intrepid seeker, have the power to make changes for that life.

You have chosen to overcome whatever injustices, difficulties, and trauma have befallen you throughout your history. You decided to find a way to change things. You've taken responsibility and taken control. The difficulties of your life have not beaten you, because you still choose to fight and learn and grow and change. I honor you, dear reader, as a courageous warrior of spirit with an unconquerable soul.

As you commence on your journey of creation, I leave you with this inspiring poem by William Ernest Henley.

Invictus

Out of the night that covers me,
Black as the pit from pole to pole,
I thank whatever gods may be
For my unconquerable soul.

In the fell clutch of circumstance
I have not winced nor cried aloud.
Under the bludgeonings of chance
My head is bloody, but unbowed.

Beyond this place of wrath and tears
Looms but the Horror of the shade,
And yet the menace of the years
Finds and shall find me unafraid.

It matters not how strait the gate,
How charged with punishments the scroll,
I am the master of my fate,
I am the captain of my soul.

Now create Your Fairytale. It may take an evening or several days or several weeks. If you get stuck, go back to the meditation exercises. Review the entries in your journal. Read some old fairytales.

Just don't give up on the process. Utilize your sacred space, your journal, and every tool that you've been given in this book. Walk away from it from time to time, if you need to. But please come back to it. Finish this work in honor of the stronger, happier person you will be on the other side of it. Don't let her down. Don't make him wait too long. Complete the magickal working called Your Fairytale.

And when you're done, take a look at the next chapter for some insights on processing this work and moving ever forward.

CHAPTER 11

꧁꧂

SO YOU'VE CREATED YOUR FAIRYTALE—BUT IS THE SPELL CAST?

If you're reading this, having gone through the steps and exercises described in this book, but have not yet created Your Fairytale, take heart, dear reader! This is a process! No one can tell you how long it should take. Everyone will deal with it a little differently, just like everyone grieves differently.

You may be delving very deeply into a scary or painful time of your life. If so, you are courageous, ambitious, and awesome! Take your time. You may even want to put the practice away for a while and pick it up again when you feel more ready to complete the project. No one can dictate to you precisely how or in what time frame to transform. Remember, you are the "captain of your soul"!

If you have completed Your Fairytale, *congratulations*! That was hard work!

If you've completed Your Fairytale, I'm extremely proud of you and right now, I want you to take a moment. Get into that meditation space and indulge all the senses. Treat yourself to a *new* taste sensation. This time, make it something you might ordinarily deny yourself, something you reserve for special occasions. This, dear reader (and now, accomplished creator), *is* a special occasion! You are celebrating!

Make yourself aware in the way that you've learned to—with all of your senses pleasantly drawn into the present moment. Have a bite or sip of your special treat and give yourself the pride that you deserve.

Think about all the effort you put into it. Think about the bravery it took to dig that deeply into your history. Give credit where credit is due.

I raise a glass to you now, my friend. Your heart, your creativity, your courage, and your transformation impress the *hell* out of me! Cheers to you, Storytelling Alchemist. Well done!

I hope that this process has brought you some enlightenment. Likely, it has.

You've now created your hypersigil. And you may already be noticing some synchronicities that signal a change in you. But has the spell been cast?

Remember that we talked about charging a hypersigil while you work on it, but there is also a final step that sends that magick out into the universe to work its wonders. Now it is time to transport your hypersigil into the realm of manifestation where it can do its work.

This is the part that makes it real magick. Take Your Fairytale, your story, your painting, your graphic novel, your musical magnum opus, and get ready for ritual.

HYPERSIGIL CHARGING EXERCISE

You know how to do this. Go to your sacred space. Make sure that it is as tidy and clean as when you first started this process. Prepare yourself a bit as well. Put on your favorite clothes and accessories. It's a special occasion.

Have at the ready a celebration snack or treat, like champagne or wine, a glass of fine, aged brandy, or sweet treats or shrimp cocktail—whatever you like. This will be reserved for the end of the ritual as a kind of toast.

Bring Your Fairytale and yourself into the sacred space and begin with your awareness meditation. You certainly have much to be thankful for now.

When you feel calm, content, and ready, pick up Your Fairytale and read it *out loud* to yourself. If it's a work of art or a piece of music, stare at it or listen to it with headphones. Remember the significance of every tiny part of it. Remember the story behind it and tell yourself the new tale of what this work of art means, *out loud.* That is very important.

As you read, speak, or gaze, you will probably cry. And that's wonderful. Read it to yourself as many times as you want. Go over it until you're blubbering. And when you feel that your emotion is at its height, keep looking at it, read its title out loud, and send it into the liminal space of creation. Set it out into the universe to do its work.

Take a deep breath. Now your hypersigil is complete. Compose yourself again with the beauty and serenity of your surroundings. Then take that sip or have that treat to celebrate your triumph! Know that your magick is traveling out to the universe and the mighty oak tree is already in the acorn. The die is cast. And you are an extremely powerful being.

After Your Fairytale is complete, you will begin to see the synchronicities that are the evidence that it is working. Acknowledge and revel in them. They are always fun to notice. You've probably transformed quite a bit just through its creation. But there may be more changes to come. Be ready for the best possible outcomes and the blessings of having worked hard on yourself.

Expect to see positive changes in yourself. And when you notice them, begin to think about how much further you can go. Begin to consider which SYTY you'll transform next. Lead to gold, baby! Can you ever have too much gold? I think not!

Next, share Your Fairytale. Share it with someone you love and trust. You can tell them the whole process and the real-life backstory if you want. You can tell them about this book and why you wrote Your Fairytale, if you like. But it's not necessary. You can simply say, "I wrote this. Will you read it? Or listen to it as I read it aloud?"

But then watch. Pay attention to their reactions. Take in the emotion that is generated in another person by Your Fairytale. (Remember, dear reader, when I said it would help others? This is it.)

Let this person shower you with compliments. They will, if you created from the heart and they love your heart. They will compliment you. They will gush.

Let the compliments come without belittling them. The only responses to these compliments—or any compliments about this work—you are permitted are 1) *total* agreement with how awesome it is, or 2) admission that you worked hard on it and are proud of the result, or 3) if you're really unable to respond in the first two ways, simply say, "Thank you!"

In other words, you will accept the compliments and not question, qualify, or doubt them in any way.

And then? Then, my dear alchemist, you will share it again. Share it in your own way. Post it on your Facebook page. Start a blog with it. Share it with whomever you deem worthy. But share it.

And, finally, *please*, I *beg* of you, brave soul, writer of wisdom, Storytelling Alchemist, share it with *me*!

You are invited to send Your Fairytale along with an explanation of the real-life story behind it and how your feelings about that real-life story have changed since the writing to StorytellingAlchemy@ gmail.com.

This is a very selfish request on my part. I love to hear the stories of those who have taken my course. It is inspiring and extremely gratifying to me to discover how my readers have changed.

Additionally—and still selfishly—I will eventually be publishing a compilation of these fairytales and other creations. If your story is chosen to be included in that publication, you will receive fabulous boons and accolades yet to be determined, credit in the new book, and my undying gratitude.

Thank you, dear reader, for joining me in Storytelling Alchemy. Your interest, participation, and support are greatly appreciated. It has been an honor and a privilege to take this journey with you.

Brightest Blessings!

SUPPLEMENTAL READINGS/ RESOURCES

Scientific Concepts
A Brief History of Nearly Everything by Bill Bryson

Magick and Will
Liber Al vel Legis or *The Book of the Law* by Aleister Crowley

The Power of Thoughts and Words
What the Bleep Do We Know? feature film available at
   whatthebleep.com.

Dream Interpretation
www.dreammoods.com/dreamdictionary
Dreams by Carl Gustav Jung and translated by R.F.C. Hull

Deities, Spirits, and Offerings

Encyclopedia of Mystics, Saints & Sages: A Guide to Asking for Protection, Wealth, Happiness, and Everything Else! by Judika Illes

Encyclopedia of Spirits: The Ultimate Guide to the Magic of Fairies, Genies, Demons, Ghosts, Gods & Goddesses by Judika Illes

Storytelling

The Story of B by Daniel Quinn

Women Who Run with the Wolves by Clarissa Pinkola Estes

Magick and Story

The Golden Bough: A Study of Magic and Religion by Sir James George Frazer

Archetypes

Collected Works of C.G. Jung, Volume 9 (Part 1): Archetypes and the Collective Unconscious by Carl Gustav Jung

Archetypes by Caroline Myss

Psychology and Alchemy

The Alchemist by Paulo Coelho

Collected Works of C.G. Jung Vol. 12: Psychology and Alchemy by Carl Gustav Jung

Sigils and Hypersigils

Book of Lies: The Disinformation Guide to Magick and the Occult edited by Richard Metzger

The Invisibles by Grant Morrison

Magickal Correspondences

www.witchipedia.com/main:correspondence-tables

The Druid Wolf Pack of Yellowstone National Park

Nature on PBS, episode available at www.pbs.org/wnet/nature/in-the-valley-of-the-wolves-the-druid-wolf-pack-story/209/

The Hero's Journey

The Hero with a Thousand Faces by Joseph Campbell

TO OUR READERS